happyfeet

happyfeet

unique knits to knock your socks off

CATHY CARRON

sixth&spring books
NEW YORK

sixth&spring books

161 Avenue of the Americas, New York, NY 10013
sixthandspringbooks.com

Editorial Director
JOY AQUILINO

Developmental Editor
LISA SILVERMAN

Yarn Editor
CHRISTINA BEHNKE

Supervising Patterns Editor
LORI STEINBERG

Editorial Assistant
JOHANNA LEVY

Contributing Patterns Editors
AMY DETJEN
RACHEL MAURER

Photography
ROSE CALLAHAN AND MARCUS TULLIS

Contributing Art Director
KAY NIEDERLITZ

Stylist and Bookings Manager
KHALIAH JONES

Hair and Makeup
ELENA LYAKIR

Vice President
TRISHA MALCOLM

Publisher
CARRIE KILMER

Creative Director
JOE VIOR

Production Manager
DAVID JOINNIDES

President
ART JOINNIDES

Chairman
JAY STEIN

Library of Congress Catalog-in-Publication Data
Happy feet: unique knits to knock your socks off /
Cathy Carron.— First Edition.
pages cm
ISBN: 978-1-936096-4-70-1
1. Knitting—Patterns. I. Title
TT825.K648 2014
746.43'2—dc23
          2013029783

Manufactured in China

1 3 5 7 9 10 8 6 4 2

First Edition

acknowledgments

"I don't knit socks; never mind design them!" That's what I told Trisha Malcolm, vice president at Sixth&Spring Books. Sock knitting is in vogue, and it seemed logical to do a collection on the heels (so to speak) of my books on hats, cowls, and cropped tops. But I wasn't persuaded at first. While I considered the idea, I recalled designing for a footwear compilation several years ago. I'd conjured a design that I could imagine myself wearing—striped, mismatched legwarmers. They ended up on the cover. Even then, I remember telling the editor, "I don't knit socks." Eventually, to Trisha's surprise, I accepted the challenge. Now, having created over forty designs, I can confidently state, "I am a sock knitter."

Why the hesitation about socks? They have to conform to a certain shape to be useful, and I love experimenting with shape. Socks are about surface design—texture and color. Another factor was time: the fine gauges of most sock yarns gobble up hours, and we wanted enough new ideas to entice the most avid sock knitter. So with some trepidation but a lot of support from the Sixth&Spring staff, the challenge began. Christina Behnke, the yarn editor, was efficient, patient, and lovely to work with. Together we waded through myriad sock yarns, fine-tuning our choices over the course of months. Overseeing the process were editorial director Joy Aquilino and developmental editor Lisa Silverman. Once again, creative director Joe Vior worked his magic on the printed page, with help from stylist Khaliah Jones and patterns editor Lori Steinberg. Thanks to you all!

As usual, I am grateful for the enthusiasm and response from the various yarn purveyors who participated. Time is always of the essence, and fabulous product came flying through the door. My only regret is the yarn not used—so much fabulous fiber and so little time and space!

contents

introduction
Get a Leg Up

This is not a book of techniques, but rather a collection of ideas—more than 40 items to knit for your "knees and toes." These projects, some with multiple variations, include just about any form of lower-leg covering a knitter might make: ankle and knee socks, legwarmers, thigh-highs, peds, sandal socks, and even a modified "sleeping bag" for your legs to use while tellie-watching. To keep you on your toes—no pun intended—a variety of sock constructions are employed as well, including tube and spiral shapes, turned heels, afterthought heels, and toe-up designs. Explore and knit the projects or use the book as a springboard for your own ideas. Most important, have fun!

In addition to the inherent bliss that comes from knitting your own socks, there's the convenience: the projects can be easily transported just about anywhere. I always keep a sock project at hand, stored in a baggie, for that purpose—I just pop it into my handbag as I make my way out the door. There's a whole sisterhood of sock knitters who roam the New York subways! If there's a downside to socks, it has to be the dreaded "second-sock-syndrome": the lack of motivation to knit two of the same thing. Personally, I don't mind: I view the first sock as the learning curve and the second sock as the "slide"—breezy and lots of fun. But if the possibility of tedium lurks, one way to banish it is simply not to knit the same sock twice! Change up the stitch pattern or coloration on the second sock; play with the design, even just a little bit. There's no rule that says socks have to match. Really.

socks that rock: the fundamentals of footwear

The amount of information out there about sock knitting can be overwhelming. Before you pick up your needles and dive into the projects in this book, here's an overview of the basics, including sock construction, sizing, and fiber choice, along with other helpful hints.

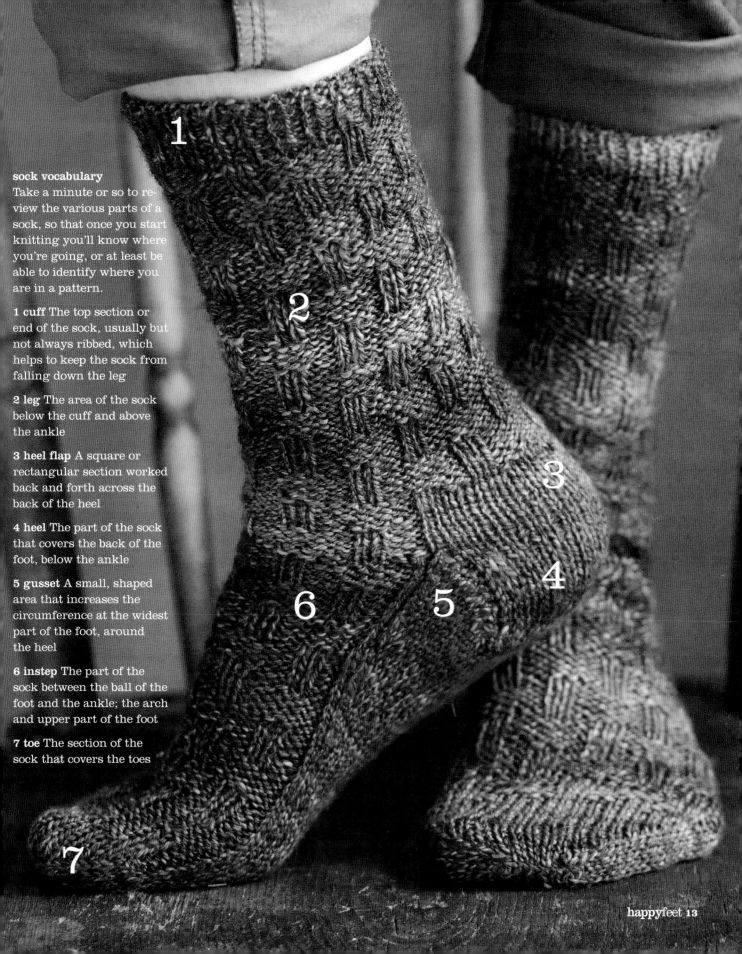

sock vocabulary

Take a minute or so to review the various parts of a sock, so that once you start knitting you'll know where you're going, or at least be able to identify where you are in a pattern.

1 cuff The top section or end of the sock, usually but not always ribbed, which helps to keep the sock from falling down the leg

2 leg The area of the sock below the cuff and above the ankle

3 heel flap A square or rectangular section worked back and forth across the back of the heel

4 heel The part of the sock that covers the back of the foot, below the ankle

5 gusset A small, shaped area that increases the circumference at the widest part of the foot, around the heel

6 instep The part of the sock between the ball of the foot and the ankle; the arch and upper part of the foot

7 toe The section of the sock that covers the toes

Solids & Stripes
(page 106)

Cuff 'Em
(page 54)

Do the Twist
(page 38)

BUILDING BLOCKS

Socks and other knitted footwear can be designed and structured in a variety of ways, but the seamless methods are by far the preferred and most common types of construction. Seamless socks are created by knitting in the round, using either double-pointed needles (dpns) or, for knitters who prefer it, two circular needles at once. A sock that has no seams, assuming it's also created without any knots or bumps, is a more comfortable and better-fitting form for the foot and is considered more hygienic and less apt to cause cuts and calluses on the skin. And, of course, it doesn't require the sewing of seams.

Almost all of the designs in this collection are constructed seamlessly. The exception is the "Solids & Stripes" slipper pattern (page 106), in which individual motifs are seamed together to form the final shape—the bulky weight and softness of the yarn specified in the pattern make the slippers appropriately safe and comfortable, and the seams are fashioned in a way that won't irritate the foot.

sock construction

Socks can be constructed in a wide variety of ways. The list below is by no means conclusive, but it includes the four main sock constructions used in this book, which are combinations of the different heel methods and different directional methods.

Don't be overwhelmed by the variety of constructions to choose from when you decide to tackle sock knitting; rather, embrace the possibilities and make a point of exploring each type of design. No doubt you will gravitate to a favorite form, as did I, after making dozens of different pairs. See "Back to Basics," on page 146, for simple examples of the first three types of construction listed here.

• top-down construction
The sock begins at the top of the leg, usually but not always with a ribbed cuff. The subsequent heel shaping can be a traditional turned heel with gusset, a tube or spiral sock, or an afterthought heel.

• toe-up construction
A bottom-up sock begins at the toe, where a small number of stitches are cast on, followed by increases to accommodate the foot. After the instep is formed, the heel can be a toe-up gusset, an afterthought construction, or a tube or spiral construction.

• afterthought heel
A sock with this type of heel can be knit either toe-up or top-down. When the knitter reaches the place where the heel is to be worked, scrap yarn is inserted (usually half the width of the sock). After the sock is completed, with either the cuff bound off or the toe grafted, the stitches are removed from the scrap yarn and picked up to work the heel.

• tube or spiral sock
A tube sock can be knit either toe-up or top-down and has no heel inserted at all. This shape usually works best when a ribbing or spiral stitch is used. It's also an optimal construction when using heavily textured yarn that can make turning a heel awkward and difficult. See "Do the Twist" on page 38 for an example of a tube sock with a spiral stitch.

THE LONG & SHORT OF IT

No sizing standard exists across sock knitting patterns. Some patterns offer a one-size-fits-all design, usually for an "average" or medium-sized sock, while others have a range of sizes such as Small, Medium, and Large. Still others express sizing in relation to comparable shoe sizes: women's shoe sizes 9–10 would be equivalent to a size Large. This variation often has to do with the type of construction used in the particular sock design. For instance, textured sock designs are dependent on the stitch multiple of the pattern used—the stitch repeat of a textured pattern might work up well or eloquently in only one size, especially if the repeat occurs over a large number of stitches. Patterns with smaller stitch repeats can accommodate a greater range of sock sizes.

Check the pattern you intend to use before you purchase yarn, to ensure you'll be able to make the socks in a size that works for you (or whomever you're making them for). The designs in this book were fashioned for women and young girls, based on the foot and leg measurements in the chart below.

All in the Family
(page 82)

SOCKS	foot length	ankle circumference	lower leg length	calf circumference
small (sizes 5–6)	9"/23cm	7"/18cm	11"/28cm	13"/33cm
medium (sizes 7–8)	10"/25.5cm	8"/20.5cm	12"/30.5cm	14"/35.5cm
large (sizes 9–10)	11"/28cm	9"/23cm	13"/33cm	15"/38cm

LEGGINGS	ankle circumference	calf circumference	knee circumference	upper thigh circumference
small	7"/18cm	13"/33cm	14"/35.5cm	15"/38cm
medium	8"/20.5cm	14"/35.5cm	15"/38cm	16"/40.5cm
large	9"/23cm	15"/38cm	16"/40.5cm	17"/43cm

MATERIAL WORLD

Yarn selection for footwear is perhaps more important than for any other item you knit, because of the relationship between overall health and foot comfort and hygiene. During the two World Wars, when women knit socks for soldiers, officials became aware of how crucial a good sock was to a man in the field: during World War I, it was said that more men were sent home for the malady known as "trench foot" than for battlefield injuries.

As a result, the military instructed voluntary agencies that supervised knitting to establish strict standards for footwear, including the institution of the concept of gauge measurement, which allowed standard-sized socks to be created in bulk and inventoried efficiently for distribution. Women were also admonished to eliminate "knots" and to refrain from using dyes that could exacerbate open wounds. (In the war's early days, some women added red monograms or even the letter "V" for victory to socks.) Even if you're not knitting socks for battle, take care to choose both a construction method and a yarn that will make your feet "happy."

There are a plethora of designated "sock yarns" on the market. These specially categorized yarns are finely spun, typically with a gauge of around 28–30 stitches per 4 inches (10 centimeters), and are often blends of fibers; for example, wool for warmth and breathability mixed with a little nylon for durability. But don't limit your options to "sock yarns"—consider any fine, natural fiber. You might even want

Forward Bend
(page 30)

Sweet Tee
(page 126)

Never Felt Better
(page 94)

Echo of Deco
(page 86)

to purchase a sample skein and knit up a swatch before deciding on a yarn for your project. Don't shy away from heavier-gauged yarns, either, especially if you live in a cold climate. They work up quickly and can make a graphic statement with either stitch patterns or colorwork.

Practically any yarn on the market can be used to make footwear. Natural fibers are preferable for their tactile quality, durability, and comfort. Synthetics can also be used, but make sure they are soft; nylon, polyesters, and acrylics can sometimes feel scratchy or prevent the skin from "breathing," leading to perspiration and possibly the formation of fungi. Natural alternative fibers such as bamboo can be used as well, but bamboo has a large amount of drape—great for sweaters, but not so much for socks. If you are considering synthetics out of concern for cleaning and care, think again and seek out superwash wool, which allows the finished item to be machine-washed, albeit in cold water only.

Finally, I would caution against using metallic yarns, even for trim, as they can irritate the skin. Again, work up a swatch to test the feel of the knitted piece.

TIPS & TRICKS

Skid-proof your slippers & socks.
This technique is used for the "Never Felt Better" slippers on page 94, but it works equally well with socks. You will need a small bottle of rubber cement, which can be purchased in drugstores or office supply and stationery stores. Generously coat the bottoms of the completely dried felted slippers with the cement (bottles come with built-in brushes). For socks, coat only the heel and toe sections; it's not necessary to cover the entire bottom. To make the sock firmer to work with and prevent the cement from oozing through, insert a (clean) shoe or sneaker, or a sole-shaped piece of cardboard. Let the socks dry completely before wearing.

Don't throw out scraps of yarn.
Keep your sock yarn scraps in a single bag, and in no time you'll have acquired enough to whip up a pair of end-of-day socks with the leftovers. They can also be used to darn or completely replace a worn-out toe or afterthought heel. In addition, sock yarn makes great tassels and pompoms.

Take special care of your handmade socks & stockings.
Make the same effort to maintain your socks that you made to knit them. Even if you used superwash wools that are billed as machine-washable, don't just toss them in. Take 3 to 5 minutes to soak your socks, then squeeze the water out without twisting, and rinse them without torturing the fibers. Lay out newspaper on a flat, non-wooden surface (as water can damage wood), place a towel over the paper, and lay the socks flat to dry. You can fold the towel over the socks and press to get more water out. I keep the socks covered with the towel if my cat is about so he doesn't choose to sleep on them; otherwise, I leave them to dry uncovered. Trust me: they will look like new, and you'll be just as excited to wear them as you were the first time. Revere your work!

Use elastic "carry-along" yarn selectively.
Elastic yarn is readily available in many colors to use as a carry-along thread, to help your socks stay up. It's a great product but should be limited primarily to thigh-high stockings or legwarmers, where you might need extra grip on the upper leg—I used it in several of those projects in this book. The elastic will change the gauge of your cuffs and make them bulkier—ribbing knitted with your main yarn should suffice to hold up an ordinary ankle or calf sock.

Handknit socks make lovely gifts.
If you've made socks for yourself and enjoyed knitting them, don't stop
there. Keep working up pairs, block them, and store them for the holidays.
The cost of yarn, for the most part, is minimal; your time, effort, and love
are the greater contributions. Such a delightful and personal present is
particularly special because most people will be surprised to receive it.
Make sock knitting a year-round habit!

gettin' ziggy

Basic stripes on the foot and zigzags on the leg
are a fun and funky combination.

WHAT YOU NEED

Yarn
Simply Sweet Satisfaction **by Be Sweet,
1¾oz/50g skeins, each approx 115yd/105m
(wool/mohair/alpaca)**
• **2 skeins in #704 blueberry (A)**
• **1 skein in #701 winter white (B)**

Needles
• **One set (4) size 4 (3.5mm) double-pointed
needles (dpns)** or size to obtain gauge

Notions
• **Stitch markers**
• **Scrap yarn**

Skill Level

●●●○

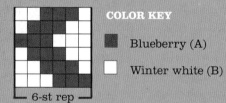

COLOR KEY

■ Blueberry (A)

□ Winter white (B)

CHEVRON STRIPED SOCKS

These socks, knit up in a warm blend of
wool, mohair, and alpaca, are simple to
make but fun and sassy to wear, thanks to
easy but eye-catching colorwork. Personal-
ize them by adding even more colors or
switching up the patterns.

SIZE

Instructions are written for size
Medium/Large (Woman's shoe sizes 8–10).

GAUGE

22 sts and 28 rnds to 4"/10cm over St st
using size 4 (3.5mm) needles. **Take time to
check gauge.**

K1, P1 RIB

(over an even number of sts)
Rnd 1 *K1, p1; rep from * around.
Rep rnd 1 for k1, p1 rib.

SOCKS

Cuff
With A, cast on 42 sts and divide evenly on
3 dpns. Pm for beg of rnd and join, being
careful not to twist sts.
Work 6 rnds in k1, p1 rib.
Next rnd Knit.
Beg chart
Rnd 1 With A and B, work 6-st rep of chart
7 times around.
Cont in this way through rnd 6. Rep rnds
1–6 until sock measures 6"/15cm from beg.
With A, knit 4 rnds.

Afterthought heel setup

Next rnd With scrap yarn, k22, sl scrap
yarn sts back to LH needle and knit them
again with A, k to end of rnd.
Next (inc) rnd With N1, k22; with N2, kfb,
k9; with N3, k9, kfb—44 sts.
Knit 3 rnds.
Beg stripe pat
Rnds 1–4 With B, knit.
Rnds 5–8 With A, knit.
Rep rnds 1–8 for stripe pat until foot
measures 6½"/16.5cm or 3"/7.5cm less
than desired sock length, end with a
rnd 4.
Toe
Arrange sts as foll: 22 sts on N1, 11 sts
each on N2 and N3. Break B. Work toe in
A only.
Rnds 1 and 2 Knit.
Rnd 3 With N1, K1, ssk, k to last 3 sts,
k2tog, k1; with N2, k1, ssk, k to end; with
N3, k to last 3 sts, k2tog, k1—4 sts dec'd.
Rnd 4 Knit.
Rep rnds 3 and 4 for 8 times more—12 sts.
Divide sts evenly on 2 dpns. Graft toe
closed using Kitchener st.
Afterthought heel
Remove scrap yarn from heel, placing sts
on 3 needles as foll: 22 sts on N1; 11 sts
each on N2 and N3. With A, work as for
toe. Graft closed using Kitchener st.❖

the net set

Easy drop-stitch leggings that extend from thigh to mid-foot mimic the look of fabulous fishnets.

the net set

WHAT YOU NEED

Yarn
Fixation **by Cascade Yarns,**
1¾oz/50g balls, each approx 100yd/91m
(cotton/elastic) 3
• **2 balls in #3794 cranberry**

Needles
• **One set (4) size 6 (4mm) double-pointed**
needles (dpns) or size to obtain gauge

Notions
• **Stitch markers**

Skill Level
●●○○

MESH LEGGINGS

The simple allover drop-stitch pattern on
these leggings is a quick and inexpensive
way to get a faux-fishnet look. It's so easy
you can do it blindfolded, and the elastic in
Cascade's **Fixation** yarn helps the leggings
stay up and hug the curves of your legs.

SIZES

Instructions are written for size Medium
(Woman's shoe sizes 7–8). Changes for
Large (Woman's shoe sizes 9–10) are in
parentheses.

FINISHED MEASUREMENTS

Circumference at upper thigh (stretched)
16 (17)"/40.5 (43)cm
Circumference at ankle (stretched)
8 (9)"/20 (23)cm
Length (unstretched) 24"/61cm

GAUGE

24 sts and 40 rnds to 4"/10cm over St st
using size 6 (4mm) needles. **Take time to**
check gauge.

STITCH GLOSSARY

Drop 1 Drop next stitch off LH needle and
allow it to unravel.

K1, P1 RIB
(over an even number of sts)
Rnd 1 *K1, p1; rep from * around.
Rep rnd 1 for k1, p1 rib.

LEGGINGS

Cast on 60 (68) sts and divide on 3 dpns.
Pm for beg of rnd and join, being careful
not to twist sts.
Rnds 1–10 Work in k1, p1 rib.
Rnd 11 *K2tog, yo; rep from * around.
Work in St st (knit every rnd) for
23"/58.5cm.
Next rnd *K1, drop 1; rep from * around—
30 (34) sts.
Rnds 1–15 Work in k1, p1 rib.
Bind off loosely in pat.✤

walking on air

Petite-but-plush slipper socks are great
for a long flight—or a relaxing day at home.

walking on air

WHAT YOU NEED

Yarn
Baby Cashmerino **by Debbie Bliss/KFI,
1¾oz/50g balls, each approx 137yd/125m
(merino wool/microfiber/cashmere)** ②
• **1 ball each in #300 black (A) and #49
taupe (B) (enough for either Tweedy or
Color Band Slippers)**

Needles
• **One set (4) size 3 (3.25mm) double-
pointed needles (dpns)** or size to obtain
gauge
• **Size 3 (3.25mm) circular needle,
16"/40cm long**

Notions
• **Stitch markers (2)**

Skill Level
● ● ○ ○

TRAVEL SLIPPERS
Here's a pair of color ideas based on a
simple travel slipper design that takes no
time to make. They are worked in the
round from the cuff down; then the bottom
is woven with a single seam up the middle
of the foot. Since they take a relatively
modest amount of yarn, it's easy to
splurge on a luxury fiber like this very
soft wool/cashmere blend, which is
strengthened with a bit of microfiber.

SIZE
Instructions are written for size
Medium/Large (Woman's shoe sizes 7–10).

FINISHED MEASUREMENTS
Length from heel to toe 9½"/24cm

GAUGE
24 sts and 36 rnds to 4"/10cm over St st
using size 3 (3.25mm) needles. **Take time
to check gauge.**

SEED STITCH
(over an even number of sts)
Rnd 1 *K1, p1; rep from * around.
Rnd 2 *P1, k1; rep from * around.
Rep rnds 1 and 2 for seed st.

K1, P1 RIB
(over an even number of sts)
Rnd 1 *K1, p1; rep from * around.
Rep rnd 1 for k1, p1 rib.

MOSS STITCH
(multiple of 4 sts)
Rnds 1 and 2 *K2, p2; rep from * around.
Rnds 3 and 4 *P2, k2; rep from * around.
Rep rnds 1–4 for moss st.

TWEEDY SLIPPERS
Cuff
*Cast on 1 st with A, cast on 1 st with B;
rep from * 26 times more for 54 sts. Divide
evenly on 3 dpns. Pm for beg of rnd and
join, being careful not to twist sts.
Rnds 1–6 *K1 with A, k1 with B; rep from
* around.
Foot
Rnd 1 With A, k27, pm, k to end of rnd.
Rnd 2 With B, work rnd 1 of seed st to 3
sts before marker, k3, slip marker (sm),
k3, work in seed st to end of rnd.
Rnd 3 With A, cont in seed st to 3 sts
before marker, k3, sm, k3, work to end
of rnd.

Rnd 4 (inc) With A, work to 3 sts before
marker, [kfb] 3 times, sm, [kfb] 3 times,
work to end of rnd—6 sts inc'd.
Rep rnds 2–4 for 7 times more, changing
to circular needle as needed—102 sts.
Sole
Rnd 1 With A, knit. Break A.
Rnds 2 and 3 With B, knit.
Rnd 4 Purl.
Rnd 5 Knit.
Rnd 6 Purl.
Rnd 7 (dec) Ssk, k last to 2 sts, k2tog—
2 sts dec'd.
Rnd 8 Purl.
Rep rnds 7 and 8 for 5 times more—90 sts.

FINISHING
Divide sts evenly on 2 ends of circular
needle and graft closed using Kitchener st.
Work second sock the same as first,
reversing the colors.

COLOR BAND SLIPPERS
Cuff
With A, cast on 54 sts. Divide evenly on 3
dpns. Pm for beg of rnd and join, being
careful not to twist sts.
Rnds 1–6 Work in k1, p1 rib.
Foot
Rnd 1 K27, pm, k to end of rnd.
Rnds 2–3 Knit.
Rnd 4 (inc) K to 3 sts before marker, [kfb]
3 times, sm, [kfb] 3 times, k to end of
rnd—6 sts inc'd.
Rnds 5–16 Rep rnds 2–4 for 4 times more,
changing to circular needle as needed—84
sts. Break A.
Rnd 17 With B, knit.
Rnds 18–19 Work in moss st to 3 sts
before marker, k3, sm, k3, cont in moss st
to end of rnd.
Rnd 20 (inc) Work in moss st to 3 sts
before marker, [kfb] 3 times, sm, [kfb] 3
times, cont in moss st to end of rnd—90 sts.
Rnds 5–16 Rep rnds 2–4 twice more—102 sts.
Sole
Work as for Tweedy Slippers, using B for
rnds 1–3 and A for rnds 4–18.

FINISHING
Finish as for Tweedy Slippers.
Work second sock the same as first,
reversing the colors.❖

forward bend

A cute cuff and variegated yarn turn simple
yoga socks into a statement for the studio.

forward bend

Yarn
Taiyo Sock **by Noro/KFI, 3½oz/100g
balls, each approx 462yd/422m
(cotton/wool/nylon/silk)**
• **1 ball in #10 green/orange/pink/turquoise
OR #30 purple/mint/black/yellow**

Needles
• **One set (4) size 3 (3.25mm) double-
pointed needles (dpns)** or size to obtain
gauge

Notions
• **Stitch marker**
• **Tapestry needle**

Skill Level
●●○○

YOGA SOCKS

Yoga socks provide a little extra warmth
whether you're working out in the heat
of the summer or the chill of the winter.
They also make a great gift and knit up
fast. Noro is a lovely yarn choice: it's
colorful and luxurious and durable, as
the nylon adds strength to the wool and
cotton.

SIZES

Instructions are written for size Small
(Woman's shoe sizes 5–6). Changes for
Medium (Woman's shoe sizes 7–8) and
Large (Woman's shoe sizes 9–10) are in
parentheses.

GAUGE

28 sts and 40 rnds to 4"/10cm over St st
using size 3 (3.25mm) needles. **Take time
to check gauge.**

K2, P2 RIB

(multiple of 4 sts)
Rnd 1 *K2, p2; rep from * around.
Rep rnd 1 for k2, p2 rib.

SOCKS

Cuff
Cast on 48 (56, 64) sts and divide on 3
dpns. Pm for beg of rnd and join, being
careful not to twist sts.
Work in k2, p2 rib for 6"/15cm. Then
work 10 (12, 14) rnds in St st.

Heel opening
Rnd 1 Bind off 24 (28, 32) sts, work in
k2, p2 rib to end of rnd.
Rnd 2 Cast on 24 (28, 32) sts, work in
k2, p2 rib to end of rnd.

Foot
Next rnd K24 (28, 32), work in k2, p2 rib
to end of rnd.
Cont to work pats as established until
foot measures 2½ (3, 3)"/6.5 (8, 8)cm from
heel opening.
Work in k2, p2 rib over all sts for
1"/2.5cm more.
Bind off in rib.

FINISHING

With tapestry needle and yarn, secure
heel corners by taking a few stitches at
each corner to reinforce. Roll cuff to RS
and tack to each corner.✦

with bells on

Colorblock legwarmers blend modern and vintage
with bell cuffs that drape over the feet.

with bells on

WHAT YOU NEED

Yarn
Lark **by Quince & Co., 1¾oz/50g hanks, each approx 134yd/123m (wool)**
• **2 hanks in #118 chanterelle (A)**
• **2 hanks in #120 gingerbread (B)**

Needles
• **One set (4) size 6 (4mm) double-pointed needles (dpns)** or size to obtain gauge
• **One set (4) size 7 (4.5mm) double-pointed needles (dpns)**

Notions
• **Stitch marker**

Skill Level
●●●○

BELL CUFF LEGWARMERS

Legwarmers are eminently useful and can be worn in a variety of ways: with skirts and dresses and over pants. Most are just tube-shaped with a stitch count gradation from ankle to thigh, but there's another, simpler way to create shaping: by increasing the needle size along the way. The yarn you are using needs to be able to comfortably span several needle sizes, like Quince & Co.'s **Lark**, used in this design. Another detail that makes these legwarmers feminine and flirty is the addition of a bell shape after the cuff—best shown off with heels, but also cute with boots or even flats.

SIZES

Instructions are written for size Medium (Woman's shoe sizes 7–8). Changes for Large (Woman's shoe sizes 9–10) are in parentheses.

FINISHED MEASUREMENTS

Circumference at calf 14 (15)"/35.5 (38)cm
Circumference at ankle 8 (9)"/20 (23)cm

GAUGES

20 sts and 28 rnds to 4"/10cm over St st using smaller needles.
32 sts and 28 rnds to 4"/10cm over relaxed k1, p1 rib using smaller needles. **Take time to check gauges.**

K1, P1 RIB

(over an even number of sts)
Rnd 1 *K1, p1; rep from * around.
Rep rnd 1 for k1, p1 rib.

K2, P2 RIB

(multiple of 4 sts)
Rnd 1 *K2, p2; rep from * around.
Rep rnd 1 for k2, p2 rib.

K2, P1 RIB

(multiple of 3 sts)
Rnd 1 *K2, p1; rep from * around.
Rep rnd 1 for k2, p1 rib.

EYELET RIB

Rnd 1 *K2tog, yo, p1; rep from * around.
Rnds 2–5 *K2, p1; rep from * around.
Rep rnds 1–5 for eyelet rib.

LEGWARMERS

Bell cuff
With A and smaller needles, cast on 84 (88) sts and divide evenly on 3 dpns. Pm and join, being careful not to twist sts. Work in k2, p2 rib for 2¼"/6cm.
Next (dec) rnd * K2tog, p2tog; rep from * around—42 (44) sts.
Work in k1, p1 rib for 4"/10cm.
Next (inc) rnd *Kfb, p1; rep from * around—63 (66) sts.
Work in k2, p1 rib for 5¾"/14.5cm. Break A. Change to larger needles.
Next rnd With B, knit.
Work one rnd more in k2, p1 rib.
Beg eyelet rib
Work rnds 1–5 of eyelet rib 15 times, then rep rnds 1–4 once more.
Bind off loosely in pat.❖

do the twist

The tube sock with a new spin: bobbles
at the top, spiraling legs, and flashy feet.

WHAT YOU NEED

Yarn
Tosh Sock **by Madelinetosh, each hank approx 395yd/361m (superwash merino wool)**
- 1 hank in silver fox (A)
- 1 hank in Edison bulb (B)

Needles
- **One set (4) size 2 (2.75mm) double-pointed needles (dpns)** or size to obtain gauge

Notions
- **Stitch marker**
- **Cable needle (cn)**

Skill Level
●●○○

SPIRAL TUBE SOCKS

The spiral sock is a classic tube sock, one of the most traditional forms of sock making. During World War II, it was introduced by the Red Cross to replace soldiers' socks that wore out on average after three weeks in the field. It was hoped that without a heel, the sock would wear more evenly. In fact, it wasn't such a hit with soldiers, who preferred socks with gusseted heels. Regardless, it remains a popular and easy-to-make sock form to this day. This design offers a twist on the classic by texture-blocking the sock, with the spiral on the leg and ribbing on the foot for a tighter, more comfortable fit.

SIZES

Instructions are written for size Small/Medium (Woman's shoe sizes 5–8). Changes for Large (Woman's shoe sizes 9–10) are in parentheses.

FINISHED MEASUREMENTS

Foot circumference 8 (9)"/20.5 (23)cm
Length from cuff to toe (unstretched) 17 (18)"/43 (45.5)cm

GAUGES

26 sts and 30 rnds to 4"/10cm over St st using size 2 (2.75mm) needles.
40 sts and 30 rnds to 4"/10cm over relaxed rib pat using size 2 (2.75mm) needles.
Take time to check gauges.

STITCH GLOSSARY

Kfb Knit into front and back of next st to inc 1 st.
MB (make bobble) Knit into the front and back of st until there are 6 loops on RH needle. Pass the first 5 loops over the last loop. Return st to LH needle and knit it.

K3, P3 SPIRAL RIB

(multiple of 6 sts plus 1)
Spiral *K3, p3; rep from *, paying no attention to beg of rnd.

SOCKS

Top
With A, cast on 48 (60) sts and divide on 3 dpns. Pm for beg of rnd and join, being careful not to twist sts.
Rnd 1 *K3, p3; rep from * around.
Rnds 2 and 3 K the knit sts and p the purl sts.
Rnd 4 *K1, MB, k1, p3; rep from * around.
Rnd 5 *K1, k1 tbl, k1, p3; rep from * around.
Rnds 6–7 Rep rnd 1.
Begin spiral rib
Setup rnd K2, kfb, *p3, k3; rep from *, end p3, remove marker—49 (61) sts.
Spiral K3, *k3, p3; rep from * for spiral rib until sock measures 6½"/16.5cm from beg. Break A. Join B.
Next (dec) rnd K2tog, knit to end of rnd—48 (60) sts.
Work in k1, p1 rib for 8½ (9½)"/21.5 (24)cm or 2"/5cm less than desired sock length.
Toe shaping
Rnd 1 and all odd-numbered rnds Knit.
Rnd 2 *K4, k2tog; rep from * around—40 (50) sts.
Rnd 4 *K3, k2tog; rep from * around—32 (40) sts.
Rnd 6 *K2, k2tog; rep from * around—24 (30) sts.
Rnd 8 *K1, k2tog; rep from * around—16 (20) sts.
Rnd 10 *K2tog; rep from * around—8 (10) sts.
Break yarn, leaving 8"/20cm tail. Thread tail through rem sts.✣

pom queen

Show off the textured legs of these knee-highs,
or let the pompoms peek out over the tops of tall boots.

pom queen

WHAT YOU NEED

Yarn
Chesapeake **by Classic Elite Yarns,
1¾oz/50g balls, each approx 103yd/94m
(organic cotton/merino)** (4)
• **5 (6) balls in #5985 mandarin orange (A)
OR #5904 scuba blue (B)**
Rainbow Elastic 3mm, **available on cards,
each approx 25yd/23m (elastic thread)**
• **1 card in #114 orange OR #60 teal**

Needles
• **One set (4) size 6 (4mm) double-pointed
needles (dpns)** or size to obtain gauge
• **Crochet hook, size F (3.75mm)**

Notions
• **Stitch marker**

Skill Level
●●●○

ST. JOHN'S WORT KNEE SOCKS
Classic Elite's **Chesapeake** yarn inspired
this design. The colors are wonderful, but
what attracted me even more was the
merino wool/organic cotton content—a
perfect mix for warm and durable socks. I
used a St. John's Wort ribbing pattern to
create a richly textured look, and to allow
the leg decreases to be worked almost
invisibly, resulting in a modern, clean look.
Contrary to appearance, these socks are not
difficult to make, since the ribbed and
rhythmic structure of St. John's Wort acts
as a guide throughout.

SIZES
Instructions are written for size
Small/Medium (Woman's shoe sizes 5–8).
Changes for Large (Woman's shoe sizes
9–10) are in parentheses.

FINISHED MEASUREMENTS
Circumference at calf (unstretched)
9 (10)"/23 (25.5)cm
Circumference at ankle (unstretched)
7 (8)"/18 (20.5)cm
Length from cuff (folded) to bottom of heel
15 (16)"/38 (40.5)cm
Length from back of heel to toe 8 (9)"/20.5
(23)cm

GAUGE
22 sts and 24 rnds to 4"/10cm over St st
using size 6 (4mm) needles. **Take time to
check gauge.**

STITCH GLOSSARY
K3po K3, pass first st worked over last 2
sts worked.

K1, P1 RIB
(over an even number of sts)
Rnd 1 *K1, p1; rep from * around.
Rep rnd 1 for k1, p1 rib.

ST. JOHN'S WORT RIB
(multiple of 4 sts)
Rnd 1 *K2, p2; rep from * around.
Rnd 2 (inc) *K1, yo, k1, p2; rep from *
around.
Rnd 3 *K3, p2; rep from * around.
Rnd 4 (dec) *K3po, p2; rep from * around.
Rep rnds 1–4 for St. John's Wort rib.

SOCKS
Cuff
With A or B, cast on 64 (72) sts and divide
on 3 dpns. Pm for beg of rnd and join,
being careful not to twist sts.
Rnds 1–6 Work in k1, p1 rib.
Rnd 7 *K2tog, yo, p2; rep from * around.
Rnds 8–20 Work in k1, p1 rib.
Rnd 21 Rep rnd 7.
Rnds 22–27 Work in k1, p1 rib.
Upper leg
Work rnds 1–4 of St. John's Wort rib 10
(11) times.
Calf shaping
Rnd 1 (dec) *K2, p2tog, k2, p2; rep from *
around—56 (63) sts.
Rnd 2 *K1, yo, k1, p1, k1, yo, k1, p2; rep
from * around.
Rnd 3 *K3, p1, k3, p2; rep from * around.
Rnd 4 * K3po, p1, k3po, p2; rep from * around.
Rnd 5 *K2, p1, k2, p2; rep from * around.
Rep rnds 2–5 for 3 times more.
Lower leg shaping
Rnd 1 (dec) *K1, yo, k1, p1, k1, yo, k1,
p2tog; rep from * around—48 (54) sts.
Rnd 2 *K3, p1; rep from * around.
Rnd 3 *K3po, p1; rep from * around.
Rnd 4 *K2, p1; rep from * around.
Rnd 5 *K1, yo, k1, p1; rep from * around.
Rep rnds 2–5 for 2 (3) times more, then
rnds 2–3 once.
Ankle shaping
Rnd 1 (dec) *K2tog, p1; rep from *
around—32 (36) sts.
Rnds 2–7 Work in k1, p1 rib.
Heel flap
Arrange sts on dpns as foll: 16 (18) sts on
N1; 8 (9) sts each on N2 and N3. Work heel
back and forth on N1 as foll:
Row 1 (RS) Knit.
Row 2 (WS) P7 (8), p2tog, p7 (8)—15 (17) sts.
Row 3 *K1, sl 1; rep from * to last st, k1.
Row 4 Purl.
Rep rows 3–4 until heel flap measures
2 (2½)"/5 (6.5)cm. Rep row 3 once more.

Instep

With RS facing and cont with N1, pick up and k 12 (14) sts along side heel flap; with N2, work in k1, p1 rib over next 15 (17) sts (1 st rem); with N3, k1, then pick up and k 12 (14) sts along side of heel flap, k the first 7 (8) sts from N1, pm for new beg of rnd—20 (23) sts on N1, 15 (17) sts on N2, 20 (23) sts on N3; 55 (63) sts in rnd.

Gusset

Rnd 1 With N1, k to last 4 sts, k2tog, k2; with N2, work in rib for 15 (17) sts; with N3, k2, ssk, k to end—2 sts dec'd.
Rnd 2 With N1, knit; with N2, work in rib for 15 (17) sts; with N3, knit.
Rep rnds 1 and 2 for 8 (10) times more—37 (41) sts.
Next rnd With N1, k to last 4 sts, k2tog, k2; with N2 and N3, work in pat to end of rnd—36 (40) sts.
Work even in pats until foot measures 2"/5cm less than desired foot length.

Toe

Sl last st on N3 to N1, sl first st on N2 to N1—18, 20 sts on N1, 9 (10) sts each on N2 and N3.
Rnd 1 Knit.
Rnd 2 With N1, k2, ssk, k to last 4 sts, k2tog, k2; with N2, k2, ssk, k to end; with N3, k to last 4 sts, k2tog, k2—4 sts dec'd.
Rnd 3 Knit.
Rep rnds 2 and 3 for 5 (6) times more—12 sts.
Divide sts evenly on 2 dpns and graft toe closed using Kitchener st.

FINISHING

Ties

With crochet hook and 1 strand each of yarn and matching elastic held tog, leaving a 4"/10cm tail at each end, make a chain about 20 (24)"/51 (61)cm long. Fold upper cuff to RS so that the 2 rows of eyelets overlap and align. Weave crochet chain in and out of these holes. Taking care not to stretch the chain, tie the ends together with a square knot. Make 4 ¾"/2cm pompoms (2 for each sock) and attach to ends of crochet chain with the tails.✤

sockets

A clever pocket at the cuff is the perfect size for
a credit card, a key, or a tiny treasure

sockets

WHAT YOU NEED

Yarn
Rialto DK **by Debbie Bliss/KFI, 1¾oz/50g balls, each approx 115yd/105m (merino wool)**
- **2 balls in #33 charcoal (A)**
- **1 ball in #44 aqua (B)**

Needles
- **One set (4) size 6 (4mm) double-pointed needles (dpns)** or size to obtain gauge

Notions
- **Stitch markers**
- **Scrap yarn**

Skill Level

●●●○

POCKET CALF SOCKS

When I run out for a quick neighborhood errand, I often just grab my keys, a credit card, and a few dollar bills. Taking a purse would be cumbersome, but bereft of pockets, I end up clutching stuff in my hands. I thought it would be nice to have socks with a secret pocket to stash my cash and card. Color blocking this design is fun, but for more security, use the same color throughout or use a subtly contrasting color for the pocket.

SIZES

Instructions are written for size Small/Medium (Woman's shoe sizes 5–8). Changes for Large (Woman's shoe sizes 9–11) are in parentheses.

FINISHED MEASUREMENTS

Foot circumference 6½ (8)"/16.5 (20)cm
Length from top to heel 11½"/29.5cm
Length from heel to toe 8¼ (10½)"/21 (27)cm

GAUGE

22 sts and 28 rnds to 4"/10cm over St st using size 6 (4mm) needles. **Take time to check gauge.**

WRAP (OR TURKISH) CAST-ON

Hold 2 dpns parallel. Beg with tail of yarn at LH side and in front of needles, wrap the working yarn around both needles for half the number of sts to cast on. (Wrap 6 times to cast on 12 sts.) Bring the yarn to the front between the needles to knit the sts on the top needle with a 3rd dpn. Rotate the needles to knit the rem sts with free dpn.

SEED STITCH

(over an even number of sts)
Rnd 1 *K1, p1, rep from * around.
Rnd 2 *P1, k1, rep from * around.
Rep rnds 1 and 2 for seed st.

K2, P2 RIB

(multiple of 4 sts)
Rnd 1 *K2, p2; rep from * around.
Rep rnd 1 for k2, p2 rib.

NOTES

1) Pair shown has 1 sock with a pocket and one sock without. To make a sock without a pocket, work as for the pocket sock from the toe to the directions to join pocket and continue in k2, p2 rib until the sock measures the same as the pocket sock to the cuff and complete as for pocket sock.

2) Socks are worked from the toe up.

SOCKS

Pocket
Note The pocket is worked from the top down.
With B, cast on 16 sts and work back and forth as foll:
Rows 1 and 2 Knit.
Row 3 K1, work row 1 of seed st over 14 sts, k1.
Row 4 P1, work row 2 of seed st over 14 sts, p1.
Next (buttonhole) row K1, work 6 sts in seed st, bind off 2 sts, work 6 sts in seed st, k1.
Next row P1, work 6 sts in seed st, cast on 2 sts, work 6 sts in seed st, p1.
Rep rows 3 and 4 until piece measures 4"/10cm. Do not bind off. Set aside.
Toe
With A, cast on 12 sts using the wrap method and divide evenly on 3 needles. Pm for beg of rnd.
Rnd 1 Knit.
Rnd 2 Kfb around—24 sts.
Rnd 3 Knit, placing 12 sts on N1 and 6 sts each on N2 and N3.
Rnd 4 With N1, k1, kfb, k to last 2 sts, kfb, k1; with N2, k1, kfb, k to end; with N3, k to last 2 sts, kfb, k1—28 sts.
Rnd 5 Knit.
Rep rnds 4 and 5 for 2 (4) times more—36 (44) sts.
Next rnd With N1, work in seed st for instep; with N2 and N3, knit.
Rep last rnd until foot measures 2 (2½)"/5 (6.5)cm less than desired length from toe to back of heel.
Afterthought heel setup
Next rnd With N1, work in seed st, with scrap yarn, k sts on N2 and N3, sl scrap

yarn sts back to LH needle and k them again with A.

Work 9 rnds in pats as established.

Next rnd Knit.

Leg

Work in k2, p2 rib for 3"/7.5cm.

Join pocket

Next rnd Work in k2, p2 rib over 10 (14) sts, k16, work in rib to end of rnd.

Next (joining) rnd Work in k2, p2 rib over 10 (14) sts, place the dpn with the pocket sts parallel to sock sts and the RS of the pocket facing the St st section of the sock; with A, k the first st on the front dpn (pocket) tog with the first st on the back dpn. Rep until all pocket sts are joined, work in rib to end of rnd.

Work in rib and St st as established for 2"/5cm. Break A.

Next rnd With B, work in pat for 2"/5cm.

Cuff

With B, work in k2, p2 rib over all sts for 5"/12.5cm.

Bind off loosely in rib.

Afterthought heel

Remove scrap yarn from heel, placing sts on 3 dpns with the 18 (22) instep sts on N1 and 9 (11) sts each on N2 and N3. With A and beg of rnd at beg of N1, work in the rnd as foll:

Rnd 1 Knit.

Rnd 2 With N1, k1, ssk, k to last 3 sts, k2tog, k1; with N2, k1, ssk, k to end; with N3, k to last 3 sts, k2tog, k1—4 sts dec'd.

Rep rnds 1 and 2 for 4 (6) times more—16 sts.

Divide sts evenly on 2 dpns. Graft heel closed using Kitchener st.

FINISHING

Sew sides of pocket in place. Sew button to correspond to buttonhole. ✤

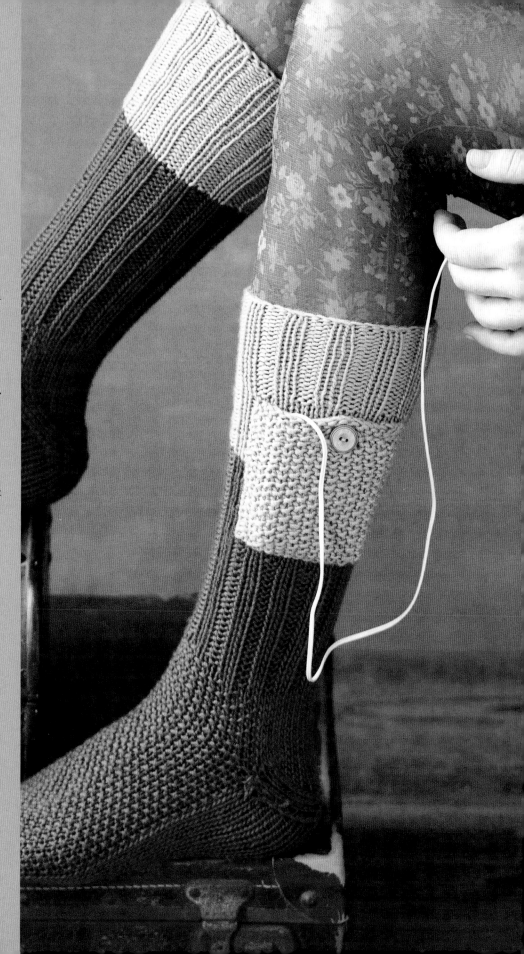

rise & shine

Paillettes at the ankles add alluring sparkle
to a simple pair of sandal footies.

rise & shine

WHAT YOU NEED

Yarn
Solemate **by Lorna's Laces,**
3½oz/100g skeins, each approx
425yd/389m (superwash merino/nylon/
viscose)
• 1 skein in #42ns carrot (version 1) OR
#0ns natural (version 2)
20mm Large Hole Paillettes **by**
Cartwright's Sequins, approx 100 in each
package
• 2 (2, 2) pkgs in gold (version 1) OR 1 (2,
2) pkgs in clear (version 2)

Needles
• One set (4) size 3 (3.25mm) double-
pointed needles (dpns) or size to obtain
gauge

Notions
• Stitch marker

Skill Level
●●●○

SEQUIN SANDAL FOOTIES

Come summer, it's great to be able to kick off your shoes and scoot around in flip-flops and sandals, but exposing your feet to the elements also puts wear and tear on your heels, which can get dried out and crack. A great way to protect them is to slip on some fun sequin-embellished "heel-sockettes."

SIZES

Instructions are written for size Small (Woman's shoe sizes 5–7). Changes for Medium (Woman's shoe sizes 8–9) and Large (Woman's shoe sizes 10–11) are in parentheses.

FINISHED MEASUREMENTS

Foot circumference 7 (8, 9)"/18 (20.5, 24)cm
Foot length 5 (5½, 6)"/12.5 (14, 15)cm

GAUGE

28 sts and 36 rnds to 4"/10cm over St st using size 3 (3.25mm) needles. **Take time to check gauge.**

STITCH GLOSSARY

PS (place sequin) Slide sequin up yarn and bring forward between 2 sts.

K1, P1 RIB

(over an even number of sts)
Rnd 1 *K1, p1; rep from * around.
Rep rnd 1 for k1, p1 rib.

FOOTIES (VERSION 1: STAND-UP SEQUINS)

Thread 64 (76, 88) sequins onto yarn and bring up as needed.
Cast on 48 (57, 66) sts loosely. Divide on 3 dpns as foll: 12 (14, 16) sts each on N1 and N3, 24 (28, 32) sts on N2. Pm for beg of rnd and join, being careful not to twist sts.
Cuff
Rnds 1–15 Knit.
Rnd 16 Purl.
Rnd 17 Knit.
Rnd 18 *K3, PS; rep from * around.
Rnds 19–21 Knit.
Rnd 22 K2, *PS, k3; rep from * around, end with k1.
Rnds 23–25 Knit.
Rnd 26 K1, *PS, k3; rep from * around, end with k2.
Rnds 27–29 Knit.
Rnds 30–33 Rep rnds 18–21.

Rnd 34 Purl.
Rnds 35 and 36 Knit.
With N3, k12 (14, 16) from N1—24 (28, 32) sts on new N1, divide rem sts evenly on 2 dpns. Work heel flap back and forth on N1 as foll:
Heel flap
Row 1 (WS) P11 (13, 15), p2tog, p11 (13, 15)—23 (27, 31) sts.
Row 2 (RS) *K1, sl 1; rep from * to last st, k1.
Next row Purl.
Rep rows 1 and 2 for 2"/5cm, end with a RS row.
Turn heel
Rnd 1 P12 (14, 16), p2tog, p1. Turn.
Rnd 2 K3, ssk, k1. Turn.
Rnd 3 P4, p2tog, p1. Turn.
Rnd 4 K5, ssk, k1. Turn.
Cont in this manner, working 1 more st before dec on each rnd, until all heel flap sts are worked—13 (15, 17) heel sts on N1.
Instep
With N1, pick up and k 12 sts along edge of heel flap; with N2, k24 (29, 34) for instep; with N3, pick up and k 12 sts along edge of heel flap, then k first 6 (7, 8) sts from N1, pm for new beg of rnd—61 (68, 75) sts.
Rnd 1 With N1, k to last 4 sts, k2tog, k2; with N2, knit; with N3, k2, ssk, k to end of rnd—2 sts dec'd.
Rnd 2 Knit.
Rep rnds 1 and 2 for 5 times more—49 (59, 63) sts.
Work even until foot measures 3½ (4, 4½)"/9 (10, 11.5)cm.
Next rnd K2tog, k to end of rnd—48 (58, 62) sts.
Next 8 rnds Work in k1, p1 rib.

FINISHING

Fold top cuff to WS along purl rnd; sew in place loosely.

FOOTIES (VERSION 2: LIE-FLAT SEQUINS)

Thread 48 (56, 64) sequins onto yarn and bring up as needed.
Cast on 48 (56, 64) sts loosely. Divide on 3 dpns as foll: 12 (14, 16) sts each on N1 and N3, 24 (28, 32) sts on N2. Pm for beg of rnd and join, being careful not to twist sts.
Cuff
Rnds 1–15 Knit.
Rnd 16 Purl.

Rnd 17 Knit.

Rnd 18 *K2, sl 1, PS, kfb, pass slipped st over last 2 sts; rep from * around.

Rnds 19–21 Knit.

Rnd 22 K1, sl 1, PS, kfb, pass slipped st over last 2 sts, *k2, sl 1, PS, kfb, pass slipped st over last 2 sts; rep from * to last st, k1.

Rnds 23–25 Knit.

Rnds 26–33 Rep rnds 18–25.

Rnd 34 Purl.

Rnds 35 and 36 Knit.

Heel flap

With N1, k24 (28, 32) for heel, turn. Working back and forth on these sts only, work heel flap as foll:

Next row (WS) P11 (13, 15), p2tog, p11 (13, 15)—23 (27, 31) sts.

Next row (RS) *K1, sl 1, rep from * to last st, k1.

Next row Purl.

Rep last 2 rows until heel flap measures 2"/5cm. Rep row 1 once more.

Turn heel

Rnd 1 P12 (14, 16), p2tog, p1. Turn.

Rnd 2 K3, ssk, k1. Turn.

Rnd 3 P4, p2tog, p1. Turn.

Rnd 4 K5, ssk, k1. Turn.

Cont in this way, working 1 more st before the dec in each row until all heel flap sts are worked—13 (15, 17) sts rem on N1.

Instep

With N1, pick up and k 12 sts along edge of heel flap; with N2, work in k1, p1 rib over next 24 (28, 32) sts; with N3, pick up and k 12 sts along edge of heel flap, then k first 6 (7, 8) sts from N1, pm for new beg of rnd—61 (67, 73) sts.

Rnd 1 K to last 4 sts on N1, k2tog, k2; with N2, work in k1, p1 rib; with N3, k2, ssk, k to end of rnd—2 sts dec'd.

Rnd 2 With N1, knit; with N2, work in k1, p1 rib; with N3, knit.

Rep rnds 1 and 2 for 5 (3, 4) times more—49 (59, 63) sts.

Work even in pats until foot measures 3½ (4, 4½)"/9 (10, 11.5)cm.

Next rnd K2tog, k to end of rnd—48 (58, 62) sts.

Work in k1, p1 rib for 8 rnds.

FINISHING

Finish as for version 1.✤

cuff 'em

Show off a beautiful variegated yarn in a simply
textured sock with a reversible foldover cuff.

cuff 'em

WHAT YOU NEED

Yarn
Hand Paint Sock Yarn Fingering
**by Misti Alpaca, 3½oz/100g hanks, each
approx 436yd/400m (alpaca/merino
wool/silk/nylon)**
• **1 hank in #HS24 tree frog**

Needles
• **One set (4) size 2 (2.75mm) double-
pointed needles (dpns)** or size to obtain
gauge

Notions
• **Stitch marker**

Skill Level
●●○○

REVERSE-INVERSE ANKLE SOCKS

There are so many lovely multicolored yarns that beckon "pick me, pick me" as you walk by in yarn shops. But they remind me of exotic house cats, who may look like any ordinary old cat, but are often muscular and more aggressive. You must take special care not to misunderstand their natures. When knitting with these colorful yarns, the phrase that comes to mind is "keep it simple"—if you don't you will obscure the fabulous lace or texture you toiled over for days, and/or distract from the coloration with too much texture. With multicolored yarns, choose a simple texture that looks good on both sides. This design employs a simple seeded rib and fashions the cuff to be folded down. If you don't care for this stitch pattern, pick one in which knitting predominates on the right side and purling on the wrong side, for contrast.

SIZES

Instructions are written for size Small/Medium (Woman's shoe sizes 5–8). Changes for Large (Woman's shoe sizes 9–10) are in parentheses.

FINISHED MEASUREMENTS

Foot circumference 7 (8)"/ 18 (20.5)cm
Length from heel to toe 9½ (10)"/24 (25.5)cm

GAUGE

32 sts and 40 rnds to 4"/10cm over St st using size 2 (2.75mm) needles. **Take time to check gauge.**

WRAP (OR TURKISH) CAST-ON

Hold 2 dpns parallel. Beg with tail of yarn at LH side and in front of needles, wrap the working yarn around both needles for half the number of sts to cast on. (Wrap 6 times to cast on 12 sts.) Bring the yarn to the front between the needles to knit the sts on the top needle with a 3rd dpn. Rotate the needles to knit the rem sts with free dpn.

ALTERNATING K2, P2 RIB

(multiple of 4 sts)
Rnds 1–10 *K2, p2; rep from * around.
Rnd 11 Knit.
Rnds 12–21 *P2, k2; rep from * around.
Rnd 22 Knit.
Rep rnds 1–22 for alternating k2, p2 rib.

SOCKS

Toe
Cast on 12 sts using the wrap method and divide evenly on 3 dpns. Pm for beg of rnd.
Rnd 1 Knit.
Rnd 2 Kfb around—24 sts.
Rnd 3 Knit, placing 12 sts on N1 and 6 sts each on N2 and N3.
Rnd 4 With N1, k1, kfb to last 2 sts, kfb, k1; with N2, k1, kfb, k to end; with N3, k to last 2 sts, kfb, k1—2 sts inc'd.
Rnd 5 Knit.
Rep rnds 4 and 5 for 8 (9) times more—56 (64) sts.
Next rnd Work rnd 1 of alternating k2, p2 rib over 28 (32) sts on N1 for instep, k to end of rnd.
Cont in this manner until piece measures 2½"/6.5cm less than desired length from heel to toe.
Gusset
Rnd 1 With N1, work instep sts in pat; with N2, k1, kfb, k to end; with N3, k to last 2 sts, kfb, k1—2 sts inc'd.
Rnd 2 Work even in alternating k2, p2 rib for instep and in St st on N2 and N3.
Rep rnds 1 and 2 for 10 (12) times more—76 (88) sts, 24 (28) each on N2 and N3.
Turn heel
Next rnd Work instep sts in pat; k27 (31), ssk, k1, turn.
Keeping N1 sts on hold for instep, work back and forth on the sts on N2 and N3 as foll:
Row 1 (WS) Sl 1, p7, p2tog, p1. Turn.
Row 2 (RS) Sl 1, k8, ssk, k1. Turn.
Row 3 Sl 1, p9, p2tog, p1. Turn.
Row 4 Sl 1, k10, ssk, k1. Turn.
Row 5 Sl 1, p11, p2tog, p1. Turn.
Cont in this way, working 1 st more before the dec on each row until all heel sts are worked and 28 (32) sts rem.
Leg
Next rnd K28 (32), pm for new beg of rnd, cont in the rnd, working alternating k2, p2 rib over all sts for 5"/12.5cm more. Bind off loosely in pat.❖

zip it

The zippers at the bottoms of these ribbed legwarmers help ensure a snug fit and sleek style.

zip it

Yarn
Ultra Alpaca Fine **by Berroco, 3⅔oz/100g hanks, each approx 433yd/400m (wool/alpaca/nylon)**
• **2 hanks in #1282 boysenberry mix**
Rainbow Elastic 3mm Bulky, **from Bryson Distributing, available on cards, each approx 25yd/23m (elastic thread)**
• **1 card in #125 burgundy**

Needles
• **One pair size 6 (4mm) needles** or size to obtain gauge
• **One set (4) size 6 (4mm) double-pointed needles (dpns)**

Notions
• **2 zippers, each 5"/12.5cm long (sample uses brass jean zippers by YKK, color #580, black)**
• **Stitch markers**
• **Sewing needle and thread (for zipper)**

Skill Level
●●●○

ANKLE ZIP LEGWARMERS

These classic ribbed legwarmers fit like a glove. The zippers on the ankles not only prove useful in getting them off and on, but also add a feminine touch to a sporty look. The design is really easy to follow—it's a progression of ribbing patterns. The legwarmers, knit in a fingering-weight yarn, take a while to make but should last a lifetime.

SIZES

Instructions are written for size Small. Changes for Medium and Large are in parentheses.

FINISHED MEASUREMENTS

Circumference at ankle 7 (8, 9)"/18 (20, 23)cm
Circumference at upper thigh 15 (16, 17)"/38 (40.5, 43)cm
Length 25 (26, 27)"/63.5 (67, 68.5)cm

GAUGE

30 sts and 40 rnds to 4"/10cm over St st using size 6 (4mm) needles. **Take time to check gauge.**

K1, P1 RIB

(over an even number of sts)
Rnd 1 *K1, p1; rep from * around.
Rep rnd 1 for k1, p1 rib.

LEGWARMERS

Ankle
With straight needles, cast on 60 (68, 76) sts.
Next row (RS) *K1, p1; rep from * to end for k1, p1 rib in rows.
Work in k1, p1 rib in rows for 5¼"/13.5cm.
Next (joining) row Place sts on 3 dpns, pm for beg of rnd and work in rnds in rib as established until piece measures 6"/15.5cm from beg.

Calf shaping
Next (inc) rnd *Kfb, p1; rep from * around—90 (102, 114) sts.
Next rnd *K2, p1; rep from * around.
K the knit sts and p the purl sts until piece measures 16 (17, 18)"/40.5 (43, 46)cm from beg.
Leg shaping
Next (inc) rnd *Kfb, k1, p1, k2, p1; rep from * around—105 (119, 133) sts.
Next rnd *K3, p1, k2, p1; rep from * around.
K the knit sts and p the purl sts until piece measures 22 (23, 24)"/56 (58.5, 61)cm from beg.
Upper Cuff
Next (dec) rnd *K2tog, k1, p1, k2, p1; rep from * around—90 (102, 114) sts.
Next rnd With yarn and elastic thread held tog, *k2, p1; rep from * around.
Rep last rnd until piece measures 25 (26, 27)"/64 (66, 68)cm from beg.
Bind off loosely in pat.

FINISHING

Pin zipper to side edges of ankle with top of zipper (opening) at cast-on edge of legwarmer and bottom of zipper even with joining rnd. Baste, then sew in place with needle and sewing thread.❖

letter perfect

These quick and comfy slippers make a great gift,
especially with the personal touch of embroidered initials.

WHAT YOU NEED

Yarn
Lamb's Pride Bulky **by Brown Sheep Company**, 4oz/113g skeins, each approx 125yd/114m (wool/mohair)
- 1 skein in #M34 Victorian pink (A)
- Small amount in #M196 teal haze (B)

Needles
- One set (4) size 10½ (6.5mm) double-pointed needles (dpns) or size to obtain gauge
- Size 10½ (6.5mm) circular needle, 24"/61cm long

Notions
- Stitch markers
- Tapestry needle
- Chalk pencil or washable marker

Skill Level
●●●○

MONOGRAM SLIPPERS

Monogrammed gifts like these slippers are special because the giver devoted extra time and effort to preparing or making them. And the personalization means they're unlikely to be "regifted"! Knit up in a chunky gauge, they're quick to make and customize: use the chart on page 144 to add an elegant scripted monogram embroidered with chain stitch.

SIZES

Instructions are written for size Small/Medium (Woman's shoe sizes 5–8). Changes for Large (Woman's shoe sizes 9–10) are in parentheses.

FINISHED MEASUREMENTS

Length from heel to toe 9¼ (10½)"/24 (26)cm

GAUGE

14 sts and 20 rnds to 4"/10cm over St st using size 10½ (6.5mm) needles. **Take time to check gauge.**

STITCH GLOSSARY

M1-open (make one open) Insert LH needle from front to back under the strand between last st worked and the next st on the LH needle; knit the strand without twisting the loop for an open increase.

WRAP (OR TURKISH) CAST-ON

Hold 2 dpns parallel. Beg with tail of yarn at LH side and in front of needles, wrap the working yarn around both needles for half the number of sts to cast on. (Wrap 6 times to cast on 12 sts.) Bring the yarn to the front between the needles to knit the sts on the top needle with a 3rd dpn. Rotate the needles to knit the rem sts with free dpn.

3-NEEDLE BIND-OFF

With 2 pieces facing each other and needles parallel, insert a 3rd needle knitwise into the first st of each needle. Wrap the yarn around the needle as if to knit, then knit these 2 stitches tog and slip them off the LH needle. *Knit the next 2 sts tog in the same way, pass the first stitch over the 2nd stitch to bind off; rep from * until required number of sts have been bound off.

SLIPPERS

Toe
With dpns and A, cast on 12 sts using the wrap method and divide evenly on 3 dpns. Pm for beg of rnd.
Rnd 1 and all odd-numbered rnds Knit.
Rnd 2 K1, M1-open, k2, M1-open, k1 (front), pm, k3 (side), pm, [kfb] twice (back), pm, k3 (side)—16 sts.
Rnd 4 K1, M1-open, k4, M1-open, k1, sm, k3, sm, k1, M1-open, k2, M1-open, k1, sm, k3—20 sts.
Rnd 6 K1, M1-open, k6, M1-open, k1, sm, k3, sm, k1, M1-open, k4, M1-open, k1, sm, k3—24 sts.

For size Large only
Rnd 8 K1, M1, k8, M1, k1 (front), sm, k3 (side), sm, k1, M1, k6, M1, k1, sm, k3—28 sts.

For both sizes
Foot
Work even in St st until piece measures 4½"/11.5cm less than desired length from heel to toe *or* for a more generic fit, work until piece measures 5 (6)"/13 (15)cm from beg—24 (28) sts.
Cuff and heel
K5 (6), turn. Cast on 6 sts. With circular needle, p29 (35), removing markers, turn. Cast on 5 (6) sts, k36 (40).
Work back and forth in welting pat as foll:
Row 1 Purl.
Row 2 Purl.
Row 3 Knit.
Row 4 Purl.
Rep rows 2–4 for welting pat 6 times more.

FINISHING

Divide sts in half, with 18 (20) sts on each end of circular needle. Fold so WS face each other. Use 3-needle bind-off to join.
Work monogram
Thread a length of color B onto tapestry needle. Use chalk pencil or washable marker to draw initial lightly on front of slipper (see chart on page 144). Embroider letter using chain stitch. ♣

dots & dashes

Add fun and flair to these simply shaped socks
with some whimsical colorwork.

dots & dashes

WHAT YOU NEED

Yarn
Simply Sweet Satisfaction **by Be Sweet,
1¾oz/50g skeins, each approx 115yd/105m
(wool/mohair/alpaca)** (4)
• **1 skein each in #701 winter white (A),
#710 espresso (B), #702 sea foam (C), and
#703 pine (D)**

Needles
• **One set (4) size 4 (3.5mm) double-pointed
needles (dpns)** or size to obtain gauge

Notions
• **Stitch markers**
• **Scrap yarn**

Skill Level

●●●○

COLORWORK SOCKS

In the bleak of winter, it's fun to sport a bit
of color on the feet. This lively four-color
design of stripes and polka dots works up
quickly with an afterthought heel.

SIZE

Instructions are written for size
Medium/Large (Woman's shoe sizes 8–10).

GAUGE

22 sts and 28 rnds to 4"/10cm over St st
using size 4 (3.5mm) needles. **Take time to
check gauge.**

K2, P2 RIB

(multiple of 4 sts)
Rnd 1 *K2, p2; rep from * around.
Rep rnd 1 for k2, p2 rib.

DOTS PATTERN

(multiple of 4 sts)
Rnd 1 *K3 A, k1 B; rep from * around.
Rnds 2–4 With A, knit.
Rnd 5 K1 A, *k1 B, k3, A; rep from *, end
k1 B, k2 A.
Rnds 6–8 With A, knit.
Rep rnds 1–8 for dots pat.

SOCKS

Cuff
With A, cast on 44 sts and divide on 3
dpns. Pm for beg of rnd and join, being
careful not to twist sts.

Work 6 rnds in k2, p2 rib.
Next rnd Knit.
Begin dots pat
Work in dots pat until sock measures
8"/20.5cm from beg, end with a row 4 or 8.
With A, knit 3 rnds.
Afterthought heel setup
Next rnd With scrap yarn, k22. Slip scrap
yarn sts back to LH needle and knit them
again with A, k to end of rnd.
Knit 2 rnds.
Begin stripes pat
Rnds 1–3 With C, knit.
Rnds 4–6 With A, knit.
Rep rnds 1–6 for stripes pat until foot
measures 5½"/14cm from scrap yarn or
3"/7.5cm less than desired sock length.
Toe
Arrange sts as foll: 22 sts on N1, 11 sts each
on N2 and N3. Break A and C and work in D.
Rnds 1 and 2 Knit.
Rnd 3 With N1, k1, ssk, k to last 3 sts,
k2tog, k1; with N2, k1, ssk, k to end; with
N3, k to last 3 sts, k2tog, k1—4 sts dec'd.
Rnd 4 Knit.
Rep rnds 3 and 4 for 8 times more—12 sts.
Divide sts evenly on 2 dpns. Graft toe
closed using Kitchener st.
Afterthought heel
Remove scrap yarn from heel, placing sts
on 3 needles as foll: 22 sts on N1; 11 sts
each on N2 and N3. With D, work as for
toe. Graft closed using Kitchener st.❖

ribs with sauce

Style meets substance when classic legwarmers
are worked in a tight gauge with zigzag ribs.

ribs with sauce

WHAT YOU NEED

Yarn
Puffin **by Quince & Co.,** 3⅛oz/100g hanks, each approx 112yd/102m (wool)
• 3 hanks in #127 cypress (A)

Needles
• **One set (4) size 9 (5.5mm) double-pointed needles (dpns)** or size to obtain gauge

Notions
• **Stitch marker**

Skill Level
●●●○

ZIGZAG LEGWARMERS

Every knitter should have a simple pattern for knee-high legwarmers handy, as they make nice quick gifts and everyone can use them. Wear them over stockings with a skirt or dress, or over boots and jeans for extra warmth. The zigzag rib used in this design can be easily substituted; just make sure your pattern's stitch multiple works. These legwarmers are made to fit snugly but still be loose enough to slip over boots. I used a smaller needle than Quince recommends for **Puffin,** to achieve a tighter and warmer knit.

SIZES
Instructions are written for size Medium. Changes for Large are in parentheses.

FINISHED MEASUREMENTS
Circumference at ankle 8 (9)"/20 (23)cm
Circumference at calf 14 (15)"/35.5 (38)cm

GAUGE
14 sts and 19 rnds to 4"/10cm over St st using size 9 (5.5mm) needles. **Take time to check gauge.**

K3, P3 RIB
(multiple of 6 sts)
Rnd 1 *K3, p3; rep from * around.
Rep rnd 1 for k3, p3 rib.

NOTE
When working the zigzag pattern, you are *not* always knitting the knit sts and purling the purl sts.

LEGWARMERS
Upper cuff
Cast on 42 (48) sts and divide evenly on 3 dpns. Pm for beg of rnd and join, being careful not to twist sts.
Rnds 1–16 Work in k3, p3 rib.
Begin spiral
Zig right (spiral) K2, kfb, p2, *k3, p3; rep from * around until sock measures 6½"/16.5cm from beg; end with a rnd that ends with k3—43 (49) sts.
Zag left (spiral) P2tog, p1, p2tog, *k3, p3; rep from * until piece measures 11"/28cm from beg; end with a rnd that ends with k3—41 (47) sts.
Zig right [Kfb] twice, k1, *p3, k3; rep from * until piece measures 15¼"/39cm from beg—43 (49) sts.
Lower cuff
Rnd 1 K2tog, k2, *p3, k3; rep from * around—42 (48) sts.
Rnds 3–9 *K3, p3; rep from * around.
Bind off in pat.✤

bob & weave

A subtly variegated yarn allows the texture
to take center stage in these bobble-and-vine-stitch anklets.

WHAT YOU NEED

Yarn
Tosh Sock **by Madelinetosh,
each hank approx 395yd/361m
(superwash merino)**
• **1 hank in well water**

Needles
• **One set (4) size 2 (3mm) double-pointed
needles (dpns)** or size to obtain gauge

Notions
• **Stitch marker**
• **Scrap yarn**

Skill Level

●●●○

BOBBLE AND VINE ANKLE SOCKS

This design is about an intricate and feminine texture that looks charming peeking
out from under a pant leg. One of my
favorite combinations is the vine stitch
with bobbles, and since the stitches are a
bit complex, it's easiest to use the afterthought heel construction. That way you
can enjoy working the texture before pick-
ing up stitches to complete the heel. If you
want to wear these with shoes, you may
want to omit the texture on the foot, as the
bobbles, while attractive, might literally
rub some wearers the wrong way!

SIZE

Instructions are written for size
Small/Medium (Woman's shoe sizes 6–8).

FINISHED MEASUREMENTS

Foot circumference 7½"/19 cm
Length from heel to toe 9½"/24cm
Length from top of cuff to bottom of heel
8½"/21.5cm

GAUGE

28 sts and 40 rnds to 4"/10cm over St st
using size 2 (2.75mm) needles. **Take time
to check gauge.**

STITCH GLOSSARY

MB (make bobble) Knit into the front and
back of st until there are 5 loops on RH
needle. Pass the first 4 loops over the last
loop. Return st to LH needle and knit it.
RT (right twist) K2tog, leaving sts on LH
needle. Knit first st again and drop both
sts from LH needle.

K1, P1 RIB

(over an even number of sts)
Rnd 1 *K1, p1; rep from * around.
Rep rnd 1 for k1, p1 rib.

BOBBLE AND VINE PATTERN

(multiple of 11 sts)
Rnd 1 *MB, k10; rep from * around.
Rnd 2 *K1 tbl, k2, k2tog, yo, RT, yo, ssk,
k2; rep from * around.
Rnd 3 Knit.
Rnd 4 *K2, k2tog, yo, k4, yo, ssk, k1; rep
from * around.

Rnd 5 Knit.
Rnd 6 *MB, k2tog, yo, k1, k2tog, yo twice,
ssk, k1, yo, ssk; rep from * around.
Rnd 7 *K1 tbl, k4, p1, k5; rep from * around.
Rnd 8 *K3, yo, ssk, k2, k2tog, yo, k2; rep
from * around.
Rnd 9 Knit.
Rnd 10 *K4, yo, ssk, k2tog, yo, k3; rep
from * around.
Rep rnds 1–10 for bobble and vine pat.

SOCKS

Cuff

Cast on 56 sts and divide on 3 dpns. Pm
for beg of rnd and join, being careful not
to twist sts.
Work 5 rnds in k1, p1 rib.
Next (dec) rnd P2tog, purl to end of rnd—
55 sts.
Begin bobbles and vines pat
Rnd 1 Work 11-st rep of bobble and vine
pat 5 times around.
Cont to work pat in this way until rnd 10
of pat is complete. Rep rnds 1–10 for 5
times more.
Afterthought heel setup
Rnd 1 With N1, work in pat as established
over next 23 sts, p2 for instep; with N2,
k14; with N3, k14; sl last 2 sts to N1.
Rnd 2 With N1, p2, work in pat over next
23 sts, p2; with N2 and N3, knit.
Rnd 3 With N1, p2, work in pat over next
23 sts, p2; with N2 and N3 with scrap yarn,
knit. Return scrap yarn sts to LH needle
and knit them again with working yarn.
Work even in pats until pat rnd 10 is complete on instep, then rep rnds 1–10 for 4
times more, keeping heel sts in St st.
Toe
Rnd 1 Kfb, k to end of rnd—56 sts.
Rnd 2 Knit.
Rnd 3 With N1, k1, ssk, k to last 3 sts,
k2tog, k1; with N2, k1, ssk, k to end; with
N3, k to last 3 sts, k2tog, k1—4 sts dec'd.
Rep rnds 2 and 3 for 10 times more—12 sts.
Divide sts evenly on 2 dpns. Graft toe
closed using Kitchener st.
Afterthought heel
Remove scrap yarn, placing 28 sts on N1
and 14 sts each on N2 and N3. Work as for
toe. Graft closed using Kitchener st. ❖

drop-dead gorgeous

Legwarmers with an undulating paisley drop-stitch
pattern strike the right balance of flirty and demure.

WHAT YOU NEED

Yarn
Fixation **by Cascade Yarns,**
1¾oz/50g balls, each approx 100yd/91m
(cotton/elastic) (3)
- **2 balls in #8176 cream (A)**
- **1 ball in #8990 black (B)**

Needles
- **One set (4) size 6 (4mm) double-pointed**
needles (dpns) or size to obtain gauge

Notions
- **Stitch markers**

Skill Level
●●●○

DROP-STITCH LEGWARMERS

A wavy, elongated paisley drop-stitch pattern adds flattering texture and peek-a-boo openwork to this pair of black-and-white legwarmers. Tall stockings like these are a nice substitute for leggings and would look great not only with dresses but with tunics as well.

SIZES

Instructions are written for size Medium (Woman's shoe sizes 7–8). Changes for Large (Woman's shoe sizes 9–10) are in parentheses.

FINISHED MEASUREMENTS

Circumference at upper thigh (stretched)
16 (17)"/40.5 (43)cm
Circumference at ankle (stretched)
8 (9)"/20 (23)cm
Length (unstretched) 20"/51cm

GAUGE

24 sts and 40 rnds to 4"/10cm over St st using size 6 (4mm) needles. **Take time to check gauge.**

STITCH GLOSSARY

Drop 1 Drop next stitch off LH needle and allow it to unravel.

2-ROW TWISTED RIB

(over an even number of sts)
Rnd 1 *K1, p1; rep from * around.
Rnd 2 *K1 tbl, p1; rep from * around.
Rep rnds 1 and 2 for 2-row twisted rib.

PAISLEY DROP STITCH

(multiple of 8 sts)
Setup rnd 1 *K2, p2, k2, p2; rep from * around.
Setup rnd 2 *K1, yo, k1, p2, k2, p2; rep from * around—9 sts in rep.
Rnds 1–7 *K3, p2, k2, p2; rep from * around.
Rnd 8 *K1, drop 1, k1, p2, k1, yo, k1, p2; rep from * around.
Rnds 9–15 *K2, p2, k3, p2; rep from * around.
Rnd 16 *K1, yo, k1, p2, k1, drop 1, k1, p2; rep from * around.
Rep rnds 1–16 for paisley drop st.

LEGWARMERS

Top cuff
With B, cast on 50 (60) sts and divide on 3 dpns. Pm for beg of rnd and join, being careful not to twist sts.
Work in 2-row twisted rib for 4"/10cm.
Next (dec) rnd *K3, k2tog tbl; rep from * around—40 (48) sts.
Break B.
Leg
With A, work setup rnds 1 and 2 of paisley drop st once, then work rnds 1–16 of paisley drop st 8 times.
Bottom cuff
Work in 2-row twisted rib for 2"/5cm.
Bind off loosely in pat.✣

adult
VERSION 1

all in the family

Matching cabled socks sized for mother, child,
and toddler are sweet and sentimental.

child
VERSION 2

toddler
VERSION 3

WHAT YOU NEED

Yarn
Alpaca Sox **by Classic Elite Yarns,
3½oz/100g hanks, each approx
450yd/412m (alpaca/merino/nylon)**
• **1 hank in #1823 strawberry for each
version (version 1 uses 300yd/275m;
version 2 uses 200yd/183m; version 3 uses
150yd/137m)**

Needles
• **One set (4) size 2 (3mm) double-pointed
needles (dpns)** or size to obtain gauge

Notions
• **Stitch marker**
• **Cable needle (cn)**

Skill Level

●●●○

MOTHER & DAUGHTER SOCKS

When I was a girl, mother-daughter
dresses were popular—a rather retro
way of bonding. Now, in a world of jeans
and T-shirts, one way to revive that
sentimental gesture is to make matching
socks. This design, worked up in a soft
alpaca blend, incorporates hugs-and-
kisses cables into the adult size, with
"warm wishes" (two-stitch cables) and
"raspberries" (bobbles) on the little
sizes—as sweet as a mother's love.

SIZES

Version 1 is written for Woman's shoe
sizes 6–10.
Version 2 is written for Child's shoe sizes
6–7.
Version 3 is written for Toddler's shoe
sizes 4–5.

FINISHED MEASUREMENTS

Adult
Foot circumference 7"/18cm
Length from heel to toe 10"/25.5cm
Length from cuff to heel 8"/20.5cm

Child
Foot circumference 5"/12.5cm
Length from heel to toe 6½"/16.5cm
Length from cuff to heel 6"/15cm

Toddler
Foot circumference 4"/10cm
Length from heel to toe 4¾"/12cm
Length from cuff to heel 4½"/11.5cm

GAUGE

32 sts and 40 rnds to 4"/10cm over St st
using size 2 (2.75mm) needles. **Take time
to check gauge.**

STITCH GLOSSARY

2-st RC Sl 1 st to cn and hold to **back**, k1,
k1 from cn.
4-st RC Sl 2 sts to cn and hold to **back**,
k2, k2 from cn.
4-st LC Sl 2 sts to cn and hold to **front**,
k2, k2 from cn.
MB (make bobble) Knit into the front
and back of st until there are 6 sts on
RH needle. Pass the first 5 sts over the
last st. Return this last st to LH needle and
knit it.

WRAP (OR TURKISH) CAST-ON

Hold 2 dpns parallel. Beg with tail of
yarn at LH side and in front of needles,
wrap the working yarn around both needles for half the number of sts to cast on.
(Wrap 6 times to cast on 12 sts.) Bring
the yarn to the front between the needles
to knit the sts on the top needle with a
3rd dpn. Rotate the needles to knit the
rem sts with free dpn.

K2, P2 RIB

(multiple of 4 sts)
Rnd 1 *K2, p2; rep from * around.
Rep rnd 1 for k2, p2 rib.

WOMAN'S SOCKS (VERSION 1)

Toe
Cast on 12 sts using the wrap method.
Divide sts evenly on 3 dpns and pm for
beg of rnd.
Rnd 1 Knit.
Rnd 2 Kfb around—24 sts.
Rnd 3 Knit, placing 12 sts on N1 and 6
sts each on N2 and N3.
Rnd 4 With N1, k1, kfb, k to last 2 sts,
kfb, k1; with N2, k1, kfb, k to end; with
N3, k to last 2 sts, kfb, k1—28 sts.
Rnd 5 Knit.
Rep rnds 4–5 for 9 times more—64 sts.
Begin chart 1
Rnd 1 Work 10-st rep of chart 1 for 3
times around, p2, k to end of rnd.
Cont to work in this way through rnd
16. Rep rnds 1–16 until foot measures
5½"/14cm or 3"/7.5cm less than desired
length from toe to heel.
Gusset
Rnd 1 With N1, cont chart pat; with N2, k1,
kfb, k to end; with N3, k to last 2 sts, kfb,
k1—2 sts inc'd.
Rnd 2 Work even in pats as established.
Rep rnds 1 and 2 for 11 times more—
88 sts in rnd, 32 on N1, 28 sts each on N2
and N3.
Turn heel
Next rnd Work 32 sts in chart pat; k31,
ssk, k1, turn.
Keeping N1 sts on hold for instep, work
back and forth on the sts on N2 and N3
as foll:
Row 1 (WS) Sl 1, p7, p2tog, p1. Turn.
Row 2 (RS) Sl 1, k8, ssk, k1. Turn.
Row 3 Sl 1, p9, p2tog, p1. Turn.
Row 4 Sl 1, k10, ssk, k1. Turn.
Cont in this way, working 1 more st be-
fore the dec on each row until all heel sts
are worked and 32 sts rem, end with a
WS row, turn.
Next rnd K32, pm for new beg of rnd,
cont in chart pat, working 10-st rep 6

times around, p2. Cont to work in this way for 3"/7.5cm more.

Cuff

Work in k2, p2 rib for 2"/5cm. Bind off loosely in rib.

CHILD'S SOCKS (VERSION 2)

Toe

Cast on 12 sts using the wrap method. Divide sts evenly on 3 dpns and pm for beg of rnd.

Work toe as for Woman's socks until there are 48 sts in rnd.

Begin chart 2

Rnd 1 Work 24 sts of chart 2, k to end. Cont to work in this way through rnd 16. Rep rnds 1–16 until foot measures 4½"/11.5cm or 2½"/6.5cm less than desired length from toe to heel.

Gusset

Rnd 1 With N1, work chart pat as established; with N2, k1, kfb, k to end; with N3, k to last 2 sts, kfb, k1—2 sts inc'd.

Rnd 2 Work even in pats as established. Rep rnds 1 and 2 for 9 times more—68 sts in rnd, 24 sts on N1, 22 sts each on N2 and N3.

Turn heel

Next rnd Work 24 sts in chart pat; k24, ssk, k1, turn.

Keeping N1 sts on hold for instep, work back and forth on the sts on N2 and N3 as foll:

Row 1 (WS) Sl 1, p7, p2tog, p1. Turn.

Row 2 (RS) Sl 1, k8, ssk, k1. Turn.

Row 3 Sl 1, p9, p2tog, p1. Turn.

Row 4 Sl 1, k10, ssk, k1. Turn.

Cont in this way, working 1 more st before the dec on each row until all heel sts are worked and 24 sts rem.

Next rnd K24, pm for new beg of rnd, cont in pats as established for 2½"/6.5cm more.

Cuff

Work in k2, p2 rib for 1"/2.5cm. Bind off loosely in pat.

TODDLER'S SOCKS (VERSION 3)

Cast on 12 sts using the wrap or Turkish cast-on method. Divide sts evenly on 3 dpns and pm for beg of rnd.

Work toe as for Woman's socks until there are 36 sts in rnd.

Begin chart 3

Rnd 1 Work 18 sts of chart 3, k to end of rnd. Cont to work in this way through rnd 16. Rep rnds 1–16 until foot measures 3"/7.5cm or 1½"/4cm less than desired length from toe to heel.

Gusset

Rnd 1 With N1, work chart pat as established; with N2, k1, kfb, k to end; with N3, k to last 2 sts, kfb, k1—2 sts inc'd.

Rnd 2 Work even in pats as established. Rep rnds 1 and 2 for 3 times more—50 sts in rnd, 18 sts on N1, 16 sts each on N2 and N3.

Turn heel

Next rnd Work 18 sts in chart pat; k18, ssk, k1, turn.

Keeping N1 sts on hold for instep, work back and forth on the sts on N2 and N3 as foll:

Row 1 (WS) Sl 1, p7, p2tog, p1. Turn.

Row 2 (RS) Sl 1, k8, ssk, k1. Turn.

Row 3 Sl 1, p9, p2tog, p1. Turn.

Row 4 Sl 1, k10, ssk, k1. Turn.

Cont in this way, working 1 more st before the dec on each row until all heel sts are worked and 18 sts rem.

Next rnd K18, pm for new beg of rnd, cont in pats for 2"/5cm more.

Cuff

Work in k2, p2 rib for 1"/2.5cm. Bind off loosely in pat. ✤

Chart 1

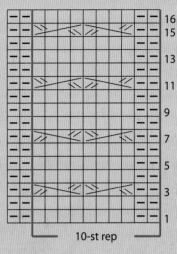

10-st rep

Chart 2

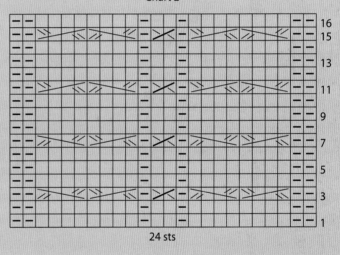

24 sts

Chart 3

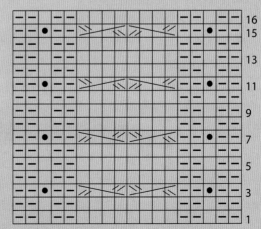

18 sts

Stitch Key

☐ K on RS, p on WS

– P on RS, k on WS

⧖ 2-st RC

⧖ 4-st RC

⧖ 4-st LC

● MB (make bobble)

echo of deco

A simple-but-striking graphic motif
gives these bulky-knit knee socks
an art deco vibe.

echo of deco

WHAT YOU NEED

Yarn
Lamb's Pride Bulky **by Brown Sheep Company**, 4oz/113g skeins, each approx 125yd/114m (wool/mohair) **5**
• 2 skeins each in #M05 onyx (A) and #M10 creme (B)

Needles
• **One set (4) size 10¼ (6.5mm) double-pointed needles (dpns)** or size to obtain gauge

Notions
• **Stitch markers**

Skill Level
●●●○

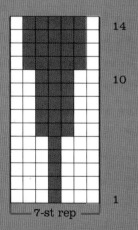

COLOR KEY

▨ Onyx (A)

☐ Snow (B)

GRAPHIC KNEE SOCKS

This past winter I went snowshoeing in Utah's Unite Hills. The team leader wore a trendy black microfiber quilted skirt—while skiing, no less. I didn't think it was possible to wear such a skirt while schussing, but it worked well and was also a fabulous look. Returning to the lodge, I immediately ordered the skirt online and sat down to design a pair of heavy woolen socks to wear with it, to achieve a total mountain look. Voila—modern Heidi! They also make cozy "house hose."

SIZE
Instructions are written for size Medium/Large (Woman's shoe sizes 7–10).

FINISHED MEASUREMENTS
Circumference at top (stretched) 16"/40.5cm
Circumference at base of ribbing 11"/28cm
Length from top of cuff to bottom of heel (unstretched, unfolded) 24"/61cm.

GAUGE
14 sts and 17 rnds to 4"/10cm over St st using size 10¼ (6.5mm) needles. **Take time to check gauge.**

SOCKS

Cuff
With A, cast on 44 sts and divide on 3 dpns. Pm for beg of rnd and join, being careful not to twist sts.
Next rnd *K2, p2; rep from * around for k2, p2 rib.
Cont in k2, p2 rib for 14"/35.5cm.
Next (dec) rnd [K2tog, k20] twice—42 sts.
Knit 5 rnds.
Begin chart
Rnd 1 Cont in St st, work 7-st rep of chart 6 times around.
Cont to work chart in this way until rnd 14 is complete.

Next (dec) rnd With B, k1; * with A, k2, ssk, k1; with B, k2tog; rep from * around, end by passing the last st of rnd over the first st of next rnd—30 sts. Break A. Cont in B only.

Ankle
Arrange sts as foll: 15 sts on N1, 7 sts on N2, 8 sts on N3.
Rnds 1 and 2 Knit.
Rnds 3–9 *K1, p1; rep from * around for k1, p1 rib.

Heel flap
Work back and forth on the 15 sts on N1 as foll:
Row 1 *K1, sl 1; rep from * across, end with k1.
Row 2 Purl.
Rep rows 1 and 2 for 4 times more.

Gusset
With N1, k2tog, k to end of needle, pick up and k 6 sts along edge of heel flap; with N2, work in rib to last 2 sts on N3, k2tog; with N3, pick up and k 6 sts along edge of heel flap, k 7 sts from N1, pm for new beg of rnd—13 sts on N1 and N3, 14 sts on N2, 40 sts in rnd.
Rnd 1 With N1, knit; with N2, work in rib as established; with N3, knit.
Rnd 2 (dec) With N1, k to last 3 sts, k2tog, k1; with N2, work in rib for 14 sts; with N3, k1, ssk, k to end—2 sts dec'd.
Rep rnds 1 and 2 for 6 times more—28 sts. Arrange sts as foll: 7 sts each on N1 and N3, 14 sts on N2.
Work even in pats as established until foot measures 2"/5cm less than desired length from heel to toe.

Toe
Rnd 1 Knit.
Rnd 2 With N1, k to last 2 sts, k2tog; with N2, k1, ssk, k to last 3 sts, k2tog, k1; with N3, k1, ssk, k to end of rnd—4 sts dec'd.
Rep rows 1 and 2 for 6 times more—12 sts. Divide sts evenly on 2 dpns. Graft toe closed using Kitchener st. ✤

layer cake

Easy-to-knit socks with triple-tiered tops are a fun way to get creative with color.

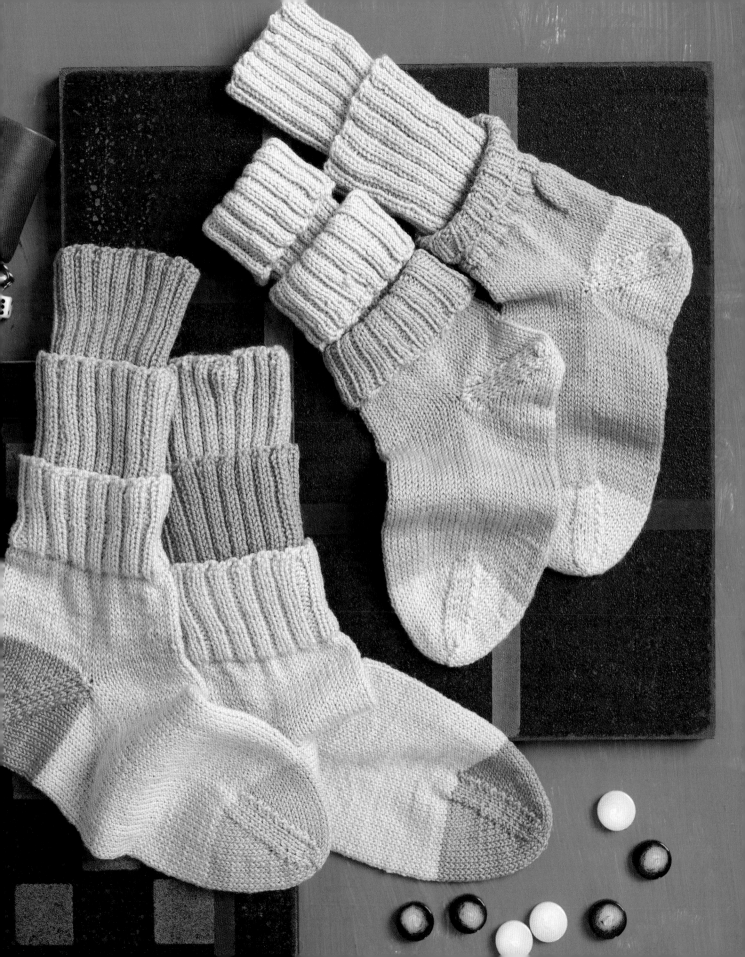

WHAT YOU NEED

Yarn
GEMS Fingering **by Louet North America,** 1¾oz/50g skeins, each approx 185yd/169m (merino wool) **(1)**
• **3-color socks: 2 skeins in #80.1012 champagne (C), 1 skein each in #80.1672 sea foam green (A) and #80.1662 bright blue (B)**
• **2-color socks: 2 skeins in #80.1512 pink panther (A and B), 1 skein in #80.1482 aqua (C)**

Needles
• **Two sets (4 each) size 3 (3.25mm) double-pointed needles (dpns)** or size to obtain gauge

Notions
• **Stitch markers**
• **Scrap yarn**

Skill Level
●●●○

TIERED CUFF SOCKS

Knitting tiers of cuffs is a way to create interest at the ankle with leftover bits of sock yarn. This afterthought-heel design allows you to focus on the cuff construction, which you work straight down to the heel, inserting a scrap yarn heel marker along the way. After the main body of the sock is completed, remove the scrap yarn, pick up the stitches, and work the heel.

SIZES

Instructions are written for size X-Small (Child). Changes for Small/Medium (Woman's shoe sizes 6–8), Large (Woman's shoe sizes 9–10), and X-Large (Woman's shoe size 11) are in parentheses.

FINISHED MEASUREMENTS

Foot circumference 6½ (7½, 8½, 9½)"/16.5 (19, 21.5, 21)cm
Length from heel to toe 5½ (7½, 9½, 11½)"/14 (19, 24, 29)cm or as desired

GAUGE

30 sts and 40 rnds to 4"/10cm over St st using size 3 (3.25mm) needles. **Take time to check gauge.**

K1, P1 RIB

(over an even number of sts)
Rnd 1 *K1, p1; rep from * around.
Rep rnd 1 for k1, p1 rib.

K2, P2 RIB

(multiple of 4 sts)
Rnd 1 *K2, p2; rep from * around.
Rep rnd 1 for k2, p2 rib.

NOTE

For 3-color socks, work second sock as for first sock, reversing A and B. For 2-color socks, use one color for both A and B.

SOCKS

First cuff
With A, cast on 48 (56, 64, 72) sts and divide on 3 dpns as foll: 24 (28, 32, 36) sts on N1; 12 (14, 16, 18) sts each on N2 and N3. Pm for beg of rnd and join, being careful not to twist sts.
Work 5"/13cm in k2, p2 rib. Set aside.

Second cuff
With B and 2nd set of dpns, work same as first cuff until piece measures 3"/7.5cm from beg.
Next (joining) rnd Slip second cuff over first cuff, lining up beg of rnds. Holding N1 parallel, join cuffs as foll: *K first st from each needle tog; rep from * until all sts are joined.
Cont with B in k2, p2 rib on 48 (56, 64, 72) sts for 1"/2.5cm more. Set aside.

Third cuff
With C, work same as for first cuff until piece measures 2"/5cm from beg.
Slip third cuff over second cuff and join as for first 2 cuffs.
Work in St st (k every rnd) for 2"/5cm more.

Afterthought heel setup
Next rnd With scrap yarn, k24 (28, 32, 36) and slip these sts back to LH needle; knit these sts again with C.
Work even in St st with C until foot measures 2½ (3½, 4½, 5)"/6.5 (9, 11.5, 12.5)cm shorter than desired length from heel to toe.

Shape toe
Rnd 1 With B, knit.
Rnd 2 With N1, k1, ssk, k to last 3 sts, k2tog, k1; with N2, k1, ssk, k to end; with N3, k to last 3 sts, k2tog, k1—4 sts dec'd.
Rnd 3 Knit.
Rep rnds 2 and 3 for 6 (8, 10, 12) times more—20 sts. Divide sts evenly on 2 dpns. Graft toe closed using Kitchener st.

Afterthought heel
Remove scrap yarn from heel, placing sts on 3 dpns: 24 (28, 32, 36) sts on N1; 12 (14, 16, 18) sts each on N2 and N3.
With B, work same as for toe. Graft heel closed using Kitchener st.❖

never felt better

Fuzzy felted house slippers hide a clever secret:
flip-flop soles that provide inner structure.

WHAT YOU NEED

Yarn

Lamb's Pride Bulky **by Brown Sheep Yarns,
3½oz/100g balls, each approx 125yd/114m
(wool/mohair)**
• **Orange slippers: 2 balls in #M110
orange you glad (A)**
• **Pink slippers: 2 balls in #M200
strawberry smoothie (A)**
La Gran Mohair **by Classic Elite Yarns
1¾oz/50g balls, each approx 106yd/97m
(mohair/wool/nylon)**
• **Orange slippers: 2 balls in #61555
tangerine (B)**
• **Pink slippers: 2 balls in #6565
pomegranate (B)**

Needles

• **One set (4) size 10½ (6.5mm) double-
pointed needles (dpns)** or size to obtain
gauge
• **Size 10½ (6.5mm) circular needle,
24"/61cm long**

Notions

• **Stitch markers (4)**
• **Tapestry needle**
• **Kitchen scissors**
• **Pair of flip-flops**
• **Rubber cement**

Skill Level

●●○○

FELTED SCUFF SLIPPERS

Here's a nifty way to create a pair of slippers with sturdy soles—by knitting and
felting a cover for flip-flops that have had
the straps removed. This design features a
covered toe; I also tried making a peep-toe
version, but exposed toes felt "chilly,"
which defeated the purpose of making
warm scuffs. Buy the cheapest pair of
rubber flip-flops that you can find—check
end-of-season sales. For these samples, I
was lucky to nab flip-flops for two dollars
a pair. And a little rubber cement makes
the felted soles skid-proof.

SIZES

Instructions are written for size Small
(Woman's shoe sizes 5–6). Changes for
Medium (7–8) and Large (9–10) are in
parentheses.

GAUGE

12 sts and 14 rnds to 4"/10cm over St st
using size 10½ (6.5mm) needles and one
strand each of A and B held together. **Take
time to check gauge.**

WRAP (OR TURKISH) CAST-ON

Hold 2 dpns parallel. Beg with tail of yarn at
LH side and in front of needles, wrap the
working yarn around both needles for half
the number of sts to cast on. (Wrap 6 times
to cast on 12 sts.) Bring the yarn to the front
between the needles to knit the sts on the top
needle with a 3rd dpn. Rotate the needles to
knit the rem sts with free dpn.

SLIPPERS

Preparation
With a heavy-duty pair of kitchen scissors,
cut and remove the straps from a pair of
flip-flops.

Sole
With one strand each of A and B held
together, cast on 12 sts for toe, using the
wrap method. Divide evenly on 3 dpns,
place marker (pm) for beg of rnd.

Rnd 1 and all odd-numbered rnds Knit.
Rnd 2 K1, M1, k2, M1, k1 (front), pm, k3
(side), pm, [kfb] twice (back), pm, k3
(side)—16 sts.
Rnd 4 K1, M1, k4, M1, k1, sl marker (sm),
k3, sm, k1, M1, k2, M1, k1, sm, k3—20
sts.
Rnd 6 K1, M1, k6, M1, k1, sm, k3, sm, k1,
M1, k4, M1, k1, sm, k3—24 sts.
Rnd 8 K1, M1, k8, M1, k1, sm, k3, sm, k1,
M1, k6, M1, k1, sm, k3—28 sts.

For size Large only
Rnd 10 K1, M1, k10, M1, k1, sm, k3, sm,
k1, M1, k8, M1, k1, sm, k3—32 sts.

For all sizes
Cont to work in St st until piece measures
4 (4½, 5½)"/10 (11.5, 14)cm from toe tip.
Weave in end at the toe.
Foot back shaping
Rnd 1 K1, [ssk, k2 (2, 3)] twice, ssk, k1,
sm, k3 (side), sm, k1, ssk, [k1 (1, 2), ssk]
twice, k1, sm, k3—22 (22, 26) sts.
Cont to work in St st until piece is
1"/2.5cm shorter than the length of the
rubber sole bottom.
Next rnd Slide the rubber sole into the
knitting and decrease for heel as foll: k1,
ssk, k3 (3, 5), ssk, k1, sm, k3, sm, k1, ssk,
k1 (3), ssk, k1, sm, k3—18 (18, 22) sts.
Next rnd Knit.
Next rnd K1, ssk, k3, ssk, k1, sm,
k3tog tbl, sm, k1, ssk, k1, ssk, k1, sm,
k3tog tbl—10 (10, 14) sts.
Next rnd K2tog around—5 (7, 7) sts.
Break yarn, leaving a 6"/15cm tail, and
thread tail through rem sts. Draw closed.
Slipper top—toe section
With one strand each of A and B held
together, cast on 6 sts. Work back and
forth.
Row 1 and all odd-numbered rows Purl.
Row 2 K1, kfb, pm, k2, pm, kfb, k1—8 sts.
Row 4 K3, sm, [kfb] twice, sm, k3—10 sts.
Row 6 K3, sm, k1, M1, k2, M1, k1, sm,
k3—12 sts.

Row 8 K3, sm, k1, M1, k4, M1, k1, sm, k3—14 sts.

Row 10 K3, sm, k1, M1, k6, M1, k1, sm, k3—16 sts.

For size Large only

Row 12 K3, sm, k1, M1, k8, M1, k1, sm, k3—18 sts.

Instep

Remove markers as you come to them and cont to work back and forth in St st until piece measures 4 (5, 6)"/10 (13, 15)cm from beg, end with a purl (WS) row.

Next row (RS) Purl.

Next row Knit.

Rep last 2 rows 4 (5, 6) times more, then purl 1 row.

Bind off loosely.

FINISHING

Beg at toe, sew slipper top to sole.

Felting

Toss the slippers in the washing machine set for a hot water wash; I usually need to do at least two cycles or washes, but each washing machine is different, so after you've completed one washing, check the slippers for fit, and if they're too large, wash them again. After they are completely felted, throw them in the dryer with a towel, which will serve to minimize noise and damage to your dryer.

Skid-proofing your slippers

Generously coat the bottom of the slippers with rubber cement and let dry.

Maintenance

To wash, toss in washing machine on cold setting if the top has kept its shape, i.e., hasn't stretched; if the top has stretched, wash in hot water to re-felt. To dry, toss in dryer on warm setting. ✤

ooh-la-lace

Feel warm and hot at the same time
in long, lacy stockings with oversize stirrups.

ooh-la-lace

WHAT YOU NEED

Yarn
Comfort Sock **by Berroco, 3½oz/100g balls, each approx 447yd/412m (nylon/acrylic)** ⓷
• 1 ball in #1734 liquorice
Rainbow Elastic 1mm, **available on cards, each approx 50yd/45m (elastic thread)**
• **2 cards in black**

Needles
• **One set (4) size 3 (3.25mm) double-pointed needles (dpns)** or size to obtain gauge

Notions
• **Stitch marker**

Skill Level
●●●○

LACY STIRRUP STOCKINGS

Black stockings and leggings are perennial classics. Black elongates the leg and can make it "disappear"—except when lace is incorporated. The lace motifs in this design were placed to accommodate the various amounts of stretch needed for each section: foot, ankle, calf, and thigh. Black can be difficult to see when knitting, but lace allows some light to filter through the piece.

SIZES
Instructions are written for size Small. Changes for Medium and Large are in parentheses.

FINISHED MEASUREMENTS
Circumference at ankle 7 (8, 9)"/18 (20.5, 23)cm
Circumference at upper thigh 15 (16, 17)"/38 (41, 43)cm
Length from upper cuff to heel opening 25"/63.5cm

GAUGE
28 sts and 40 rnds to 4"/10cm over St st using size 3 (3.25mm) needles. **Take time to check gauge.**

K1, P1 RIB
(over an even number of sts)
Rnd 1 *K1, p1; rep from * around.
Rep rnd 1 for k1, p1 rib.

CAMPANULA STITCH
(multiple of 5 sts)
Rnds 1–4 *K3, p2; rep from * around.
Rnd 5 *Yo, SK2P, yo, p2; rep from * around.
Rep rnds 1–5 for campanula st.

HORIZONTAL PICOT PATTERN
(multiple of 3 sts)
Setup rnds 1 and 2 *K1, p2; rep from * around.
Rnd 1 *K1, p2tog, yo; rep from * around.
Rnds 2–5 *K1, p2; rep from * around.
Rep rnds 1–5 for horizontal picot pat.

HORIZONTAL MESH PATTERN
(over an even number of sts)
Rnd 1 *K2tog, yo; rep from * around, end k0 (1, 0).
Rnd 2 Knit.
Rnd 3 Purl.
Rnd 4 Knit.
Rnd 5 *Yo, k2tog; rep from * around, end k0 (1, 0).
Rnds 6–8 Rep rnds 2–4.
Rep rnds 1–8 for horizontal mesh pat.

PICOT RIB
(multiple of 4 sts)
Rnds 1–6 *K2, p2; rep from * around.
Rnd 7 *K2tog, yo, p2; rep from * around.
Rep rnds 1–7 for picot rib.

STOCKINGS
Cast on 48 (52, 56) sts and divide on 3 dpns. Pm for beg of rnd and join, being careful not to twist sts.
Rnd 1 Work in k1, p1 rib for 4¾ (5, 5¼)"/12 (13, 13.5)cm.
Heel opening
Next rnd Bind off 24 (26, 28) sts, work to end of rnd.
Next rnd Cast on 24 (26, 28) sts, work to end of rnd.
Work in k1, p1 rib for 4"/10cm.
Calf shaping
Rnds 1 and 2 Purl.
Rnd 3 Knit.
Rnd 4 *K4, M1; rep from * around—60 (65, 70) sts.
Work in campanula st for 4 (5, 5)"/10 (12.5, 12.5)cm.
Next 2 rnds Purl.
Next rnd *K4, kfb; rep from * around—72 (78, 84) sts.
Purl 2 rnds.
Work in horizontal picot pat for 3"/7.5cm, end with a rnd 5.
Purl 2 rnds.
Next rnd *K5, kfb; rep from * around—84 (91, 98) sts.
Purl 2 rnds.
Next rnd Knit.
Calf
Work rnds 1–8 of horizontal mesh pat 6 times.
Upper leg
Rnds 1–2 Purl.
Rnds 3–4 Knit.
Rnd 5 *K2tog, yo; rep from * around, end with k0 (1, 0).
Rnds 6–7 Knit.
Rnds 8–9 Purl.
Rnd 10 Knit.
Rnd 11 *K6, kfb; rep from * around—96 (104, 112) sts.
Work rnds 1–7 of picot rib 8 times.
Thigh
With 1 strand each of yarn and elastic held tog, work as foll:
Rnd 1 Knit.
Rnd 2 *K6, k2tog; rep from * around—84 (91, 98) sts.
Work in k1, p1 rib for 2"/5cm.
Bind off loosely in pat.❖

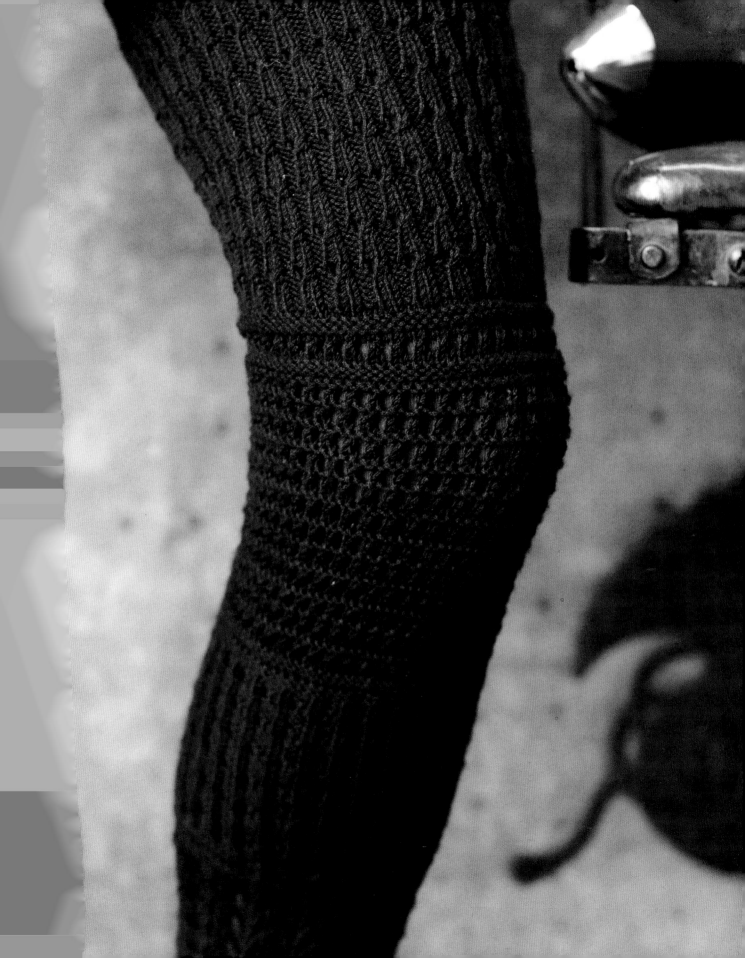

festive feet

Add some extra cheer to every season with these whimsical holiday-themed ankle socks.

festive feet

WHAT YOU NEED

Yarn
Heritage **by Cascade Yarns,
3⅕oz/100g hanks, each approx
437yd/400m (merino wool/nylon)** [1]
• **Valentine's Day: 1 hank each in #5618
snow (A), #5619 Christmas red (B), and
#5616 fuchsia (C)**
• **Fourth of July: 1 hank each in #5615
blue (A), #5619 Christmas red (B), and
#5618 snow (C)**
• **Halloween: 1 hank each in #5641 mango
(A) and #5601 night (B)**

Needles
• **One set (4) size 2 (2.75mm) double-
pointed needles (dpns)** or size to obtain
gauge

Notions
• **Stitch marker**
• **Scrap yarn**

Skill Level
●●●○

HOLIDAY ANKLE SOCKS

When my sister and I were growing up,
my mother, a fabulous seamstress, made us
holiday-appropriate dresses: simple pastel
shifts with scalloped edges for Easter; dark
velvets with lace collars for Christmas.
St. Patrick's Day dresses would be kelly-
green cotton with white collars, but as we
marched out the door she'd "safety" pin on
an orange bow, saying, "The green is for
your father [who was Catholic], but the
orange is for me [Protestant]"—no small
gesture in our Catholic neighborhood in
the Boston suburbs! When my own kids
were little I'd scoop up holiday socks at
store checkout counters. The kids loved
them, and we still occasionally come across
a pair while cleaning out drawers.

Holidays come and go quickly, but we
should celebrate them in knitting regardless. Here's a trio of quick-to-make sock
designs with easy afterthought heels and
fairly simple holiday motifs for Halloween,
the Fourth of July, and Valentine's Day.

NOTE
The sock pattern is the same for all ver-
sions, with the exception of the charts.

SIZES
Instructions are written for size
Small/Medium (Woman's shoe sizes 6–8).
Changes for Large (Woman's shoe sizes
9–10) are in parentheses.

FINISHED MEASUREMENTS
Foot circumference 8 (8½)"/20.5 (22)cm
Length from heel to toe 9 (10¼)"/23
(26)cm
Length from cuff to bottom of heel
7½ (8)"/19 (20.5)cm

GAUGE
32 sts and 42 rnds to 4"/10cm over St st
using size 2 (2.75mm) needles. **Take time
to check gauge.**

K1, P1 RIB
(over an even number of sts)
Rnd 1 *K1, p1; rep from * around.
Rep rnd 1 for k1, p1 rib.

VALENTINE'S DAY AND FOURTH OF
JULY SOCKS
Cuff
With A, cast on 64 (72) sts and divide on
3 dpns. Pm for beg of rnd and join, being

careful not to twist sts. Work in k1, p1
rib for 1"/2.5cm. Knit 2 rnds.
Beg chart
Note For first Valentine's Day sock use
heart chart 1, for second Valentine's Day
sock use heart chart 2.
Next rnd Work 8-st chart rep 8 (9) times
around.
Cont in this way until chart is complete.
Cont in St st with A only until sock measures 4¾ (5½)"/12 (14)cm from beg edge.
Afterthought heel setup
Next rnd With scrap yarn, k32 (36), slip
scrap yarn sts back to LH needle and
knit them again with A.
Foot
Cont in St st until foot measures 3
(3¼)"/7.5 (8.5)cm shorter than the desired
length from heel to toe, or, for a more
generic fit, work until piece measures
4 (4½)"/10 (11.5)cm from scrap yarn.
Toe
Arrange sts on dpns as foll: 32 (36) sts
on N1; 16 (18) sts each on N2 and N3.
Rnd 1 With B (or C for second Valentine's
Day sock), knit.
Rnd 2 With N1, k1, ssk, k to last 3 sts,
k2tog, k1; with N2, k1, ssk, k to end; with
N3, k to last 3 sts, k2tog, k1—4 sts dec'd.
Rnd 3 Knit.
Rep rnds 2 and 3 for 7 (8) times more—
20 sts.
Divide sts evenly on 2 dpns. Graft toe
closed using Kitchener st.
Afterthought heel
Carefully remove scrap yarn for heel and
place sts on 3 dpns as for toe. With A for
Valentine's Day socks or B for Fourth of
July socks, work same as for toe. Graft
heel closed using Kitchener st.

HALLOWEEN SOCKS
With A for bat sock or B for skull sock,
cast on 64 (72) sts and divide on 3 dpns.
Pm for beg of rnd and join, being careful
not to twist sts. Work in k1, p1 rib for
1"/2.5cm. Knit 2 rnds.
Beg chart
Next rnd Work 16-st (18-st) chart rep 4
times around.
Cont in this way until chart is complete.

Work as for Valentine's Day sock to toe.
Shape toe as for Valentine's Day sock,
working in stripe pat as foll: For bat sock,
*1 rnd B, 1 rnd A; for skull sock, *1 rnd A,
1 rnd B; rep from * to end for stripe pat.
Work afterthought heel in same manner.❖

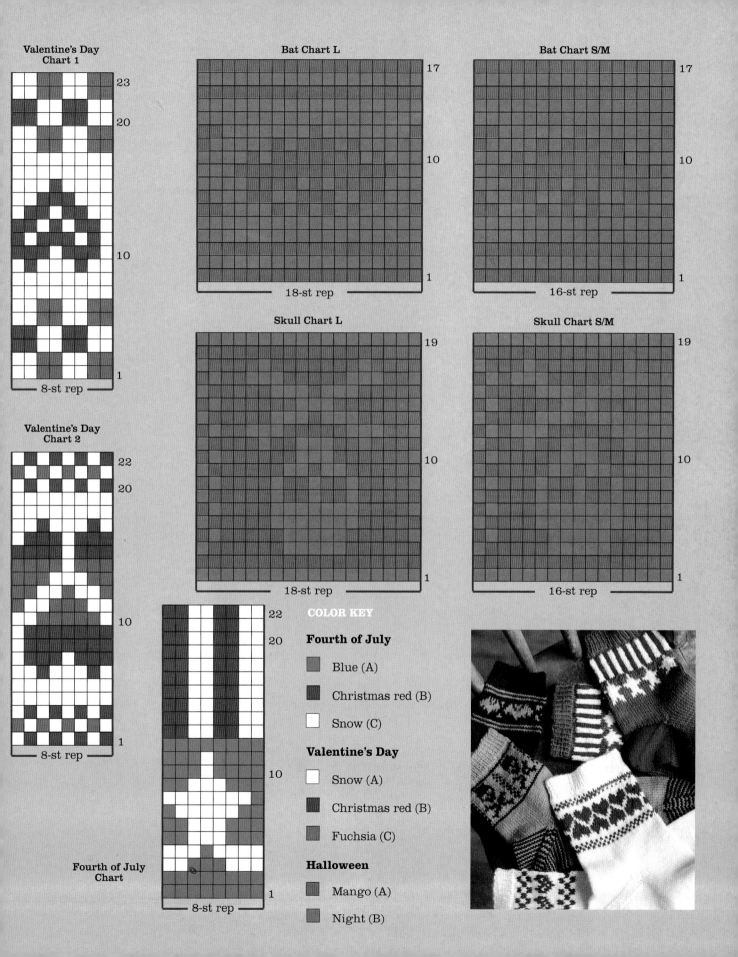

Valentine's Day Chart 1

23
20
10
1

8-st rep

Valentine's Day Chart 2

22
20
10
1

8-st rep

Bat Chart L

17
10
1

18-st rep

Bat Chart S/M

17
10
1

16-st rep

Skull Chart L

19
10
1

18-st rep

Skull Chart S/M

19
10
1

16-st rep

Fourth of July Chart

22
20
10
1

8-st rep

COLOR KEY

Fourth of July

Blue (A)

Christmas red (B)

Snow (C)

Valentine's Day

Snow (A)

Christmas red (B)

Fuchsia (C)

Halloween

Mango (A)

Night (B)

solids & stripes

Whether knit in bright colors or soft neutrals,
chunky booties are the ultimate in warmth and comfort.

WHAT YOU NEED

Yarn
Outer **by Spud & Chloe, 3½oz/100g hanks, each approx 60yd/55m (superwash wool/cotton)**
• **2 hanks in #7217 wave OR #7219 buoy**
• **Striped booties: 1 hank each in #7200 soapstone (A) and #7201 flannel (B)**

Needles
• **One set (4) size 10½ (6.5mm) double-pointed needles (dpns)** or size to obtain gauge

Notions
• **Locking stitch markers or safety pins (2)**

Skill Level
●●●○

CHUNKY BOOTIES

Spud & Chloe's **Outer** is perfect for footwear; its bulky blend of superwash wool and organic cotton makes it hard-wearing, easy to maintain, and warm and cozy to the touch. These booties are incredibly simple to make; each pair requires three squares, two large (6-inch) and one small (2½-inch) for each bootie. Just the ticket for that quick, "I-didn't-forget" holiday gift.

SIZES

Instructions are written for size Medium/Large (Woman's shoe sizes 7–10).

FINISHED MEASUREMENTS

Foot circumference 8½"/21.5cm
Length from heel to toe 9"/23cm

GAUGES

12 sts and 14 rnds to 4"/10cm over St st using size 10½ (6.5mm) needles.
Large square = 6"/15cm.
Small square = 2½"/6.5cm.
Take time to check gauges.

WRAP (OR TURKISH) CAST-ON

Hold 2 dpns parallel. Beg with tail of yarn at LH side and in front of needles, wrap the working yarn around both needles for half the number of sts to cast on. (Wrap 6 times to cast on 12 sts.) Bring the yarn to the front between the needles to knit the sts on the top needle with a 3rd dpn. Rotate the needles to knit the rem sts with free dpn.

STRIPE PATTERN A

2 rnds A, 2 rnds B.
Rep these 4 rnds for stripe pat A.

STRIPE PATTERN B

2 rnds B, 2 rnds A.
Rep these 4 rnds for stripe pat B.

NOTE

Each bootie is made up of 2 large squares and 1 small square.

ONE-COLOR BOOTIES

Large square (make 2)
Cast on 12 sts using the wrap method.
Rnd 1 [K3, pm] 3 times, k3.
Rnd 2 [Kfb, k to 1 st before marker, kfb, sm] 4 times—8 sts inc'd.

Rnd 3 Knit.
Rep rnds 2 and 3 for 5 times more—60 sts.
Bind off loosely.
Small square
Cast on 12 sts using the wrap method.
Rnd 1 [K3, pm] 3 times, k3.
Rnd 2 [Kfb, k to 1 st before marker, kfb, sm] 4 times—8 sts inc'd.
Rnd 3 Knit.
Rep rnds 2 and 3 once more—28 sts.
Bind off loosely.

FINISHING

Fold the two large squares in half with the WS facing inward. Place them side-to-side, creating a "V" with the point facing you. With a tapestry needle, and taking the outermost loop of the edge sts, whip stitch together the center seam on both the front facing you and the back. Next, with locking markers or safety pins, pin one corner of the small square to one outer point of the joined squares and pin the opposite corner to the center intersection of the larger squares. Sew the small square to one side of the large square on each side. Make a bunch of extra wrap stitches at the instep to reinforce the bootie.

STRIPED BOOTIES

Large square A
With A, cast on 12 sts using the wrap method.
Work as for one-color bootie, working in stripe pat A.
Large square B
With A, cast on 12 sts using the wrap method.
Work as for one-color bootie, working in stripe pat B.
Small square A
With A, cast on 12 sts using the wrap method. Work as for one-color bootie, working in stripe pat A.
Small square B
With A, cast on 12 sts using the wrap method. Work as for one-color bootie, working in stripe pat B.

FINISHING

Finish as for one-color bootie, using 1 large square A and 1 large square B for the bottom. Sew on small square so that the edge color is different from the edge color of the large square.✤

garden variety

Mix and match these three pieces
to keep your feet toasty and dry in outdoor clogs.

garden variety

WHAT YOU NEED

Yarn

Koigu Painter's Palette Premium Merino (KPPPM) **by Koigu Wool Designs,** 1¾oz/50g hanks, each approx 175yd/160m **(merino wool)** (1)
- 1 hank each in #P163 blue/green/orange **(A)** and #P161 purple/yellow/aqua **(B) OR**
- 1 hank each in #P136 aqua/green/yellow **(A)** and #P139 plum/green/yellow **(B)**

Needles
- **One set (4) size 3 (3.25mm) double-pointed needles (dpns)** or size to obtain gauge
- **Size 3 (3.25mm) circular needle, 16"/40cm long**

Notions
- **Stitch marker**

Skill Level

●●○○

CLOG SOCK SET

When working in the yard, digging and gardening, I prefer wearing clogs. They keep my feet above what is usually damp ground and provide lots of stability in varied terrain. I always wear socks with the clogs, too, so I made a set of footwear—crew socks, ruffled peds, and heelless footies—in the same yarn, to layer as needed, weather dependent. Just for fun, two different but complementary color-ways in Koigu's fabulous varigated wool were used for the left and right of each pair—have fun and mix and match.

SIZE

Instructions are written for Medium/Large (Woman's shoe sizes 7–10).

FINISHED MEASUREMENTS

Foot circumference 8"/20.5cm
Length from heel to toe for calf socks and ankle socks 9"/23cm
Length from heel to toe for heelless socks 4½"/11.5cm
Length from cuff to bottom of heel for calf socks 9"/23cm
Length from cuff to bottom of heel for ankle socks and heelless socks 3"/7.5cm

GAUGE

28 sts and 36 rnds to 4"/10cm over St st using size 3 (3.25mm) needles. **Take time to check gauge.**

K2, P2 RIB

(multiple of 4 sts)
Rnd 1 *K2, p2; rep from * around.
Rep rnd 1 for k2, p2 rib.

MOSS STITCH

(multiple of 4 sts)
Rnds 1 and 2 *K2, p2; rep from * around.
Rnds 3 and 4 *P2, k2; rep from * around.
Rep rnds 1–4 for moss st.

NOTES

1) Two hanks of yarn are enough to make one set.
2) The crew socks and peds are constructed cuff-down.

CREW SOCKS

(make 1 in each color)
Cuff
Cast on 56 sts and divide on 3 dpns as foll: 14 sts each on N1 and N3; 28 sts on N2.

Pm for beg of rnd and join, being careful not to twist sts.
Work in k2, p2 rib for 6"/15cm.
Work in St st for 1"/2.5cm more.

Heel flap
Setup rnd K42, turn. You will now work back and forth on the 28 sts on N2.
Row 1 (WS) P13, p2tog, p13—27 sts.
Row 2 (RS) *K1, sl 1; rep from *, end k1.
Row 3 (WS) Purl.
Rep rows 2 and 3 until heel flap measures 2"/5cm. Rep row 2 once more.

Turn heel
Row 1 P14, p2tog, p1. Turn.
Row 2 K3, ssk, k1. Turn.
Row 3 P4, p2tog, p1. Turn.
Row 4 K5, ssk, k1. Turn.
Cont in this manner, working 1 st more before the dec on every row until all sts have been worked and 15 sts rem on N2, end with a WS row.
Next rnd With N1, pick up and k 12 sts along edge of heel flap; with N2, k28 for instep; with N3, pick up and k 12 sts along edge of heel flap, then k8 from N1, pm for new beg of rnd—67 sts in rnd; 19 sts on N1, 28 sts on N2, 20 sts on N3.

Gusset
Rnd 1 (dec) With N1, k to last 4 sts, k2tog, k2; with N2, knit; with N3, k2, ssk, k to end—2 sts dec'd.
Rnd 2 Knit.
Rep rnds 1 and 2 for 5 times more—55 sts.
Next rnd Kfb, then k to end—56 sts.
Cont in St st until foot measures 7"/18cm or 2"/5cm less than desired length from heel to toe.

Toe shaping
Rnd 1 With N1, k to last 4 sts, k2tog, k2; with N2, k2, ssk, k to last 4 sts, k2tog, k2; with N3, k2, ssk, k to end—52 sts.
Rnd 2 Knit.
Rep rnds 1 and 2 for 11 times more—8 sts.
Divide sts evenly on 2 dpns. Graft toe closed using Kitchener st.

RUFFLED PEDS

(make 1 in each color)
Cuff
With circular needle, cast on 112 sts. Pm for beg of rnd and join, being careful not to twist sts.
Rnd 1 Knit.
Rnd 2 Change to dpns and *k2tog; rep from * around—56 sts.
Divide sts on 3 dpns as foll: 14 sts each on N1 and N3, 28 sts on N2.

Work 9 rnds in k1, p1 rib.

Heel flap

Setup rnd Work in rib for 42 sts, turn. You will now work back and forth on the 28 sts on N2.

Work heel flap and turn heel as for crew sock.

Gusset

With N1, pick up and k 12 sts along edge of heel flap; with N2 work in moss st over 28 sts for instep; with N3, pick up and k 12 sts along edge of heel flap, then k8 from N1, pm for new beg of rnd.

Rnd 1 With N1, k to last 4 sts, k2tog, k2; with N2, work in moss st; with N3, k2, ssk, k to end—2 sts dec'd.

Rnd 2 Knit.

Rep rnds 1 and 2 for 5 times more—55 sts.

Next rnd Kfb, knit to end—56 sts.

Work even in pats until foot measures 7"/18cm or 2"/5cm less than desired length from heel to toe.

Complete as for crew sock.

HEELLESS FOOTIES

(make 1 in each color)

Cast on 56 sts and divide on 3 dpns. Pm for beg of rnd and join, being careful not to twist sts.

Work in k2, p2 rib for 3"/8cm.

Next rnd Bind off 28 sts, work in k2, p2 rib to end.

Next rnd Cast on 28 sts, work in k2, p2 rib to end.

Work in k2, p2 rib for 4½"/11.5cm.

Bind off loosely in rib. ❖

gather 'round

Socks with pretty gathered cuffs and seed-stitch feet
blend comfy and cute for relaxed days at home.

gather 'round

Yarn
Nadeshiko **by Noro/KFI**, 3½oz/100g skeins, each approx 142yd/130m (angora/wool/silk)
• **2 skeins in #3 (green/gray)**

Needles
• **One set (4) size 10½ (6.5mm) double-pointed needles (dpns)** or size to obtain gauge

Notions
• **Stitch marker**

Skill Level
●●○○

HOUSE SOCKS

Comfortable socks to wear around the house are indispensible, no matter the season, and the right yarn is key for warmth, attractiveness, and durability. Look for blends with wool and a strengthening fiber such as silk or acrylic. Noro's **Nadeshiko** is a luxurious choice, with its angora/wool/silk content and sophisticated coloration. And these can be whipped up in no time, because of the bulky gauge.

SIZE

Instructions are written for size Medium/Large (Woman's shoe sizes 7–10).

FINISHED MEASUREMENTS

Foot circumference 7½"/19cm
Length from heel to toe 8½"/21.5cm
Length from cuff to heel 11"/28cm

GAUGE

12 sts and 20 rnds to 4½"/10cm over St st using size 10½ (6.5mm) needles. **Take time to check gauge.**

TWISTED RIB

(over an even number of sts)
Rnd 1 *K1 tbl, p1; rep from * around.
Rep rnd 1 for twisted rib.

SEED STITCH

(over an even number of sts)
Rnd 1 *K1, p1, rep from * around.
Rnd 2 *P1, k1, rep from * around.
Rep rnds 1 and 2 for seed st.

SOCKS

Cuff
Cast on 24 sts and divide evenly on 3 dpns. Place marker (pm) for beg of rnd and join, being careful not to twist sts.
Rnds 1–5 Work in twisted rib.

Rnd 6 Purl.
Rnd 7 Kfb around—48 sts.
Rnds 8–12 Knit.
Rnd 13 K2tog around—24 sts.
Rnds 14–15 Purl.
Rnds 16–33 Rep rnds 7–15 twice more. Work in twisted rib for 7 rnds.

Heel flap
Arrange sts as foll: 12 sts on N1, 6 sts each on N2 and N3.
Work the 12 sts on N1 back and forth as foll:
Row 1 (RS) K5, kfb, k6—13 sts.
Row 2 (WS) Purl.
Row 3 *K1, sl 1; rep from * end, k1.
Rep rows 2 and 3 until heel flap measures 2½"/6.5cm. Then rep row 2 once more.

Gusset
Next rnd With N1, k5, k2tog, k6, pick up and k 6 sts along edge of heel flap; with N2, work 12 sts in twisted rib as established; with N3, pick up and k 6 sts along edge of heel flap, then k6 from N1, pm for new beg of rnd—36 sts, 12 on each dpn.
Rnd 1 With N1, k to last 3 sts, k2tog, k1; with N2, work in seed st; with N3, k1, ssk, k to end—2 sts dec'd.
Rnd 2 With N1, knit; with N2, cont in seed st; with N3, knit.
Rep rnds 1 and 2 for 5 times more—24 sts.
Keeping sts on N2 in seed st as established, work even in seed st over all sts until foot measures 6½"/16.5cm, or 2"/5cm less than desired length from heel to toe.
Rnd 1 With N1, k to last 3 sts, k2tog, k1; with N2, k1, ssk, k to last 3 sts, k2tog, k1; with N3, k1, ssk, k to end—4 sts dec'd.
Rnd 2 Knit.
Rep rnds 1 and 2 twice more—12 sts.
Divide sts on 2 dpns. Graft sts closed using Kitchener st.✣

twinkle toes

Take basic sandals and make them sparkle
with bead-and-flower-embellished toe huggers.

WHAT YOU NEED

Yarn
Cotton Fine **by Brown Sheep Company,
1¾oz/50g skeins, each approx 222yd/203m
(cotton/merino wool)**
• **1 skein in #CF810 cherry moon (version
1) OR #CF844 celery leaves (version 2) OR
#CF310 wild orange (version 3)**

Needles
• **One set (4) size 2 (2.75mm) double-
pointed needles (dpns)** or size to obtain
gauge

Notions
• **#6 glass seed beads (6/0), approx 40g
(samples use Fire Mountain Gems
Dynamites™, 1 box in silver-lined silver
for version 1 OR transparent aqua for
version 2 OR silver-lined gold for
version 3)**

Skill Level

●●●○

SANDAL TOE HUGGERS

Every foot needs a little summertime
bling. These toe-kinis can be worn with
flip-flops or thong sandals, which best
reveal the beadwork. They also protect
your feet from dryness and the sun in
warmer weather.

SIZES

Instructions are written for size
Small/Medium (Woman's shoe sizes 5–8).
Changes for Large (Woman's shoe sizes
9–10) are in parentheses.

FINISHED MEASUREMENTS

Circumference (approx) 8 (9)"/20 (23)cm
Foot length 3¼ (3½)"/8 (9)cm

GAUGE

28 sts and 44 rnds to 4"/10cm over St st
using size 2 (2.75mm) dpns. **Take time to
check gauge.**

STITCH GLOSSARY

K1-bead Slide bead close to RH needle tip;
knit next st so that bead is on front loop
of st.
K2tog-bead Slide bead close to RH needle
tip; k2tog so that bead is on front loop
of st.
Kfb Knit into front and back of next st to
inc 1 st.
Kbf Knit into back and front of next st to
inc 1 st.

K2, P2 RIB

(multiple of 4 sts)
Rnd 1 *K2, p2; rep from * around.
Rep rnd 1 for k2, p2 rib.

SEED STITCH

(over an even number of sts)
Rnd 1 *K1, p1; rep from * around.
Rnd 2 P the knit sts and k the purl sts.
Rep rnd 2 for seed st.

TOE HUGGERS (VERSION 1)

String 120 (140) beads onto yarn, bring-
ing up a single bead as needed.
Cast on 48 (56) sts and divide on 3 dpns
as foll: 24 (28) sts on N1, 12 (14) sts each
on N2 and N3. Pm for beg of rnd and
join, being careful not to twist sts.
Rnds 1–4 Purl.
Rnd 5 Knit.
Rnd 6 *K1, k1-bead; rep from * to end of
N1, k to end of rnd.
Rnd 7 *K1, k1 tbl; rep from * to end of
N1, k to end of rnd.
Rnd 8 Knit.
Rnd 9 *K1-bead, k1; rep from * to end of
N1, k to end of rnd.
Rnd 10 *K1 tbl, k1; rep from * to end of
N1, k to end of rnd.
Rnd 11 Knit.
Rep rnds 6–11 for 4 times more.
Toe
For right foot only
Setup rnd K24 (28), pm for new beg
of rnd.

For both feet
Rnd 1 K10 (11), p28 (34), k10 (11).
Rnd 2 Purl.
Rnds 3–4 Rep rnds 1 and 2.
Rnd 5 K11, bind off next 28 (34) sts, k to
end—20 (22) sts.
Joining rnd 6 With N1, k8; with N2,
k1 (2), kfb, kfb, k1 (2); with N3, k8—22
(24) sts.
Rnds 7–14 Knit.
Rnds 15–16 Purl.
Bind off loosely.

FINISHING

Beaded toe flower
Cut a 30"/76cm strand of yarn. With
tapestry needle, thread strand through
fabric from WS to RS at base of toe.
String 17 beads onto yarn and secure
loop with a stitch where yarn comes out
of fabric. Make another 7 loops (8 loops
total).

TOE HUGGERS (VERSION 2)

String 42 (48) beads onto yarn, bringing
up a single bead as needed.
Cast on 52 (60) sts and divide on 3 dpns.
Pm for beg of rnd and join, being careful
not to twist sts.
Rnds 1–2 P2, *k2, p2, rep from *, end k2
for k2, p2 rib.
Rnd 3 [P2, k2tog-bead] 7 (8) times, work
in rib as established to end of rnd.
Rnd 4 [P2, kbf] 7 (8) times, work in rib to
end of rnd.
Rnds 5–7 Cont in k2, p2 rib.
Rnds 8–33 Rep rnds 3–7 five times more.
Toe
For right foot only
Setup rnd Work in rib for 26 (20) sts, pm
for new beg of rnd.

For both feet
Rnd 34 Work in rib for 12 sts, bind off 28
(32) sts, work in rib to end of rnd.

Divide sts evenly on 3 dpns. Pm and join to work in the rnd.
Cont in k2, p2 rib for 6 rnds more. Bind off loosely in pat.

FINISHING
Work beaded toe flower as for version 1.

TOE HUGGERS (VERSION 3)
String 54 (63) beads onto yarn, bringing up a single bead as needed.
Cast on 48 (58) sts and divide on 3 dpns as foll: 24 (27) sts on N1, 12 (16) sts on N2, 12 (15) sts on N3. Pm for beg of rnd and join, being careful not to twist sts.

Foot
Rnds 1–3 Work in seed st.
Rnd 4 Knit.
Rnd 5 [Yo, k3, pass the yo over the 3 sts] 8 (9) times, k to end of rnd.
Rnd 6 Knit.
Rnd 7 [K1, k1-bead, k1] 8 (9) times, k to end of rnd.
Rnd 8 Knit, working beaded sts as k1 tbl.
Rnds 9–32 Rep rnds 5–8 for 6 times more.
Rnd 33 Rep rnd 5.
Rnd 34 Knit.

Toe
For right foot only
Setup rnd K24 (27), pm for new beg of rnd.

For both feet
Rnds 1–3 Work in seed st.
Rnd 4 Work 12 sts in pat, bind off next 24 (34) sts, work to end of rnd—24 sts. Divide sts evenly on 3 dpns and pm for beg of rnd.
Work in seed st for 9 rnds. Bind off loosely in pat.

FINISHING
Work beaded toe flower as for version 1. ✤

dyed in the wool

A rustic handspun and hand-dyed yarn is the inspiration for homey basketweave socks.

dyed in the wool

WHAT YOU NEED

Yarn
Handspun Merino **by Tanglewood Fiber Creations**, varying-weight hanks, each approx 365yd/334m (superwash merino)
• **1 hank in driftwood**

Needles
• **One set (4) size 3 (3.25mm) double-pointed needles (dpns)** or size to obtain gauge

Notions
• **Stitch markers**

Skill Level
●●●○

VARIEGATED ANKLE SOCKS

Tanglewood Fiber Creations' yarn inspired these cozy socks. Owner Trisha Anderson and her spinners produce luscious mixtures of brown and tan, dyeing and spinning fibers like artists mix paint. The warm tones beg to be knitted in fun basketweave patterns. The made-to-order hanks vary in size; you'll need about 365 yards for a pair of these socks.

SIZE

Instructions are written for size Medium/Large (Woman's shoe sizes 8–10).

FINISHED MEASUREMENTS

Foot circumference 7"/18cm
Length from top to heel 8"/20.5cm
Length from heel to toe 11"/28cm

GAUGE

27 sts and 32 rnds to 4"/10cm over basketweave pat using size 3 (3.25mm) needles. **Take time to check gauge.**

STITCH GLOSSARY

Kfb Knit into front and back of next st to inc 1 st.

BASKETWEAVE PATTERN

(multiple of 8 sts)
Rnds 1–4 *K2, p6; rep from * around.
Rnd 5 *K2, p2; rep from * around.
Rnds 6–9 P4, *k2, p6; rep from * to last 4 sts, k2, p2.
Rnd 10 Rep rnd 5.
Rep rnds 1–10 for basketweave pat.

SOCKS

Cuff
Cast on 48 sts and divide on 3 dpns as foll: 24 sts on N1, 12 sts each on N2 and N3.

Pm for beg of rnd and join, being careful not to twist sts.
Next 8 rnds *K1, p1; rep from * around for k1, p1 rib.
Knit 1 rnd.
Begin basketweave pat
Work rnds 1–10 of basketweave pat 5 times. Sock measures approx 7"/18cm from beg.
Heel flap
Next rnd With N1, work in basketweave pat as established; with N2 and N3, knit. Turn to work back and forth on the 24 sts on N2 and N3 only as foll:
Row 1 (WS) Purl.
Row 2 (RS) Kfb, *k1, sl 1; rep from * across, end k1—25 sts.
Row 3 Purl.
Row 4 *K1, sl 1; rep from * across, end k1. Rep rows 3 and 4 until heel flap measures 2"/5cm, rep row 3 once more.
Gusset
Next rnd With N1, k2tog, k23, pick up and k 12 sts along edge of heel flap; with N2, k24; with N3, pick up and k 12 sts along edge of heel flap, then k12 sts from N1, pm for new beg of rnd—72 sts, 24 sts on each dpn.
Rnd 1 With N1, k to last 3 sts, k2tog, k1; with N2, work in basketweave pat; with N3, k1, ssk, k to end—2 sts dec'd.
Rnd 2 Work in pats as established.
Rep rnds 1 and 2 for 12 times more—48 sts. Work even in pats until foot measures 2"/5cm less than desired length from heel to toe.
Toe shaping
Rnd 1 With N1, k to last 3 sts, k2tog, k1; with N2, k1, ssk, k to last 3 sts, k2tog, k1; with N3, k to last 3 sts, k2tog, k1—4 sts dec'd.
Rnd 2 Knit.
Rep rnds 1 and 2 for 9 times more—8 sts. Divide sts evenly on 2 dpns. Graft toe closed using Kitchener st.❖

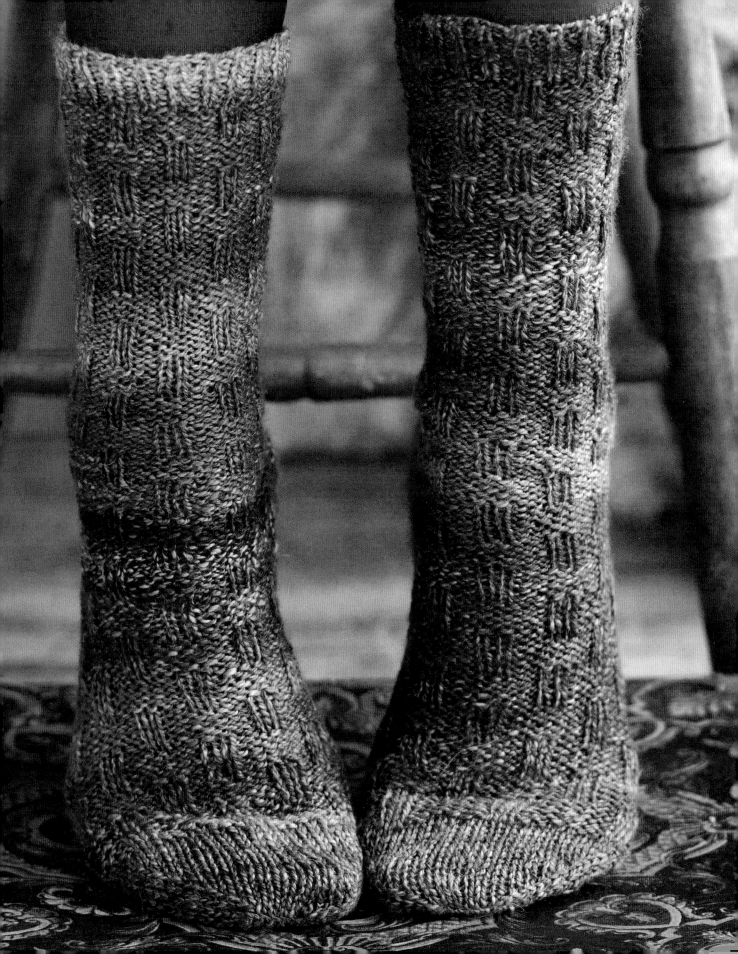

sweet tee

A sturdy but breathable T-shirt yarn makes fun
footwear for working out or chilling out.

sweet tee

WHAT YOU NEED

Yarn
T-shirt **by Be Sweet, varying-weight skeins (cotton/viscose/elastane)** (6)
• **3½oz/100g (approx 120yd/110m) in purple**

Needles
• **One set (4) size 11 (8mm) double-pointed needles (dpns)** or size to obtain gauge

Notions
• **Stitch marker**

Skill Level

●●○○

SUMMER SOCKS

I find working with unusual fibers, like T-shirt yarn, to be fun and a nice break from the usual worsted wool. It can pose substantial design challenges in achieving the desired shape, especially for footwear: it's not exactly easy to manipulate. However, this cotton jersey fiber is perfect for warm-weather wear; it's sturdy and cool to the touch. Here's a summer slipper that's great to wear around the pool or just lounging about. It's worth the effort!

SIZE

Instructions are written for size Small/Medium (Woman's shoe sizes 5–8). Changes for Large (Woman's shoe sizes 9–10) are in parentheses.

FINISHED MEASUREMENTS

Foot circumference 8 (9¼)"/20.5 (24)cm
Length from top to heel 6"/15cm
Length from heel to toe 4"/10cm

GAUGE

10 sts and 15 rnds to 4"/10cm over St st using size 11 (8mm) needles. **Take time to check gauge.**

SOCKS

Cuff
Cast on 20 (24) sts and divide on 3 dpns as foll: 7 (8) sts each on N1 and N3, and 6 (8) sts on N2. Pm for beg of rnd and join, being careful not to twist sts.
Rnd 1 Purl.
Rnd 2 Knit.
Rnd 3 Purl.
Rnds 4–8 Knit.

Heel flap
Work back and forth on the 7 (8) sts on N1 only.
Rnds 1–8 Work in St st.
Gusset
Next rnd With N1, k7 (8), then pick up and k 5 sts along edge of heel flap; with N2, k13 (16); with N3, pick up and k 5 sts along edge of heel flap, then k3 (4) from N1, pm for new beg of rnd—29 (34) sts; 8 (9) sts each on N1 and N3, 13 (16) sts on N2.
Knit 1 rnd.
Rnd 1 With N1, k to last 3 sts, k2tog, k1; with N2, knit; with N3, k1, ssk, k to end—2 sts dec'd.
Rnd 2 Knit.
Rep rnds 1 and 2 for 4 times more—19 (24) sts rem.
Work even in St st for 10 rnds.
Rnd 11 Purl.
Rnd 12 Knit.
Rnd 13 Purl.
Bind off loosely.❖

in the bag

A snuggly sack in super-bulky wool keeps your legs
warm and cozy when you're curled up on the couch.

WHAT YOU NEED

Yarn
Magnum **by Cascade Yarns,**
8¾oz/250g hanks, each approx 123yd/113m
(wool) (6)
• **2 hanks each in #9421 blue Hawaii (A)**
and #9416 camel (E)
• **1 hank each in #0010 ecru (B),**
#8012 doeskin heather (C), and #8013
walnut heather (D)

Needles
• **Size 15 (10mm) circular needle,**
29"/74cm long, or size to obtain gauge
• **Spare size 15 (10mm) needle, for**
3-needle bind-off

Notions
• **Stitch marker**

Skill Level
●●○○

FOOT SNUGGLY SACK

How many times have you tossed an afghan over your legs on a chilly night while watching TV, only to have the backs not quite covered? The ripple design of this bag is a riff on the traditional ripple afghan, reconfigured to fit your lower body. My guess is that once the family sees what you're up to, everyone will want their own.

SIZE
One size fits most.

FINISHED MEASUREMENTS
Circumference at hip 45"/114cm
Length 41"/104cm

GAUGE
10 sts and 11 rnds to 4"/10cm over ripple pat 2 using size 15 (10mm) needle. **Take time to check gauge.**

RIPPLE PATTERN 1 (GARTER ST BASE)
(multiple of 14 sts)
Rnd 1 Purl.
Rnd 2 Kfb, k4, ssk, k2tog, k4, *kfb twice, k4, ssk, k2tog, k4; rep from * to last st.
Rnd 3 Purl.
Rnd 4 Rep rnd 2.
Rep rnds 1–4 for ripple pat 1.

RIPPLE PATTERN 2 (ST ST BASE)
(multiple of 14 sts)
Rnd 1 Knit.
Rnd 2 Kfb, k4, ssk, k2tog, k4, *kfb twice, k4, ssk, k2tog, k4; rep from * to last st, kfb.
Rnd 3 Knit.
Rnd 4 Rep rnd 2.
Rep rnds 1–4 for ripple pat 2.

3-NEEDLE BIND-OFF
With two pieces facing each other and the needles parallel, insert a third needle knitwise into the first stitch of each needle. Wrap the yarn around the needle as if to knit, then knit these two stitches together and slip them off the LH needle.

*Knit the next two stitches together in the same way, slip the first stitch over the second stitch to bind off. Rep from * across.

BAG
Upper legs
With A, cast on 112 sts and divide on 3 dpns. Pm for beg of rnd and join, being careful not to twist sts.
Rnds 1–4 Work in ripple pat 1. Cut A.
Rnds 5–12 With D, work 8 rnds in ripple pat 2. Cut yarn.
Rep rnds 5–12 for 8 times more, working 8 rnds each color in foll sequence: B, E, A, C, B, E, D, C.
Lower legs
Rnd 1 (dec) With C, k3, [k2tog tbl, k4, k2tog tbl] 7 times, k2tog tbl, k4, k2tog tbl, k3—96 sts. Cut C.
Rnd 2 Kfb, k3, ssk, k2tog, k3, [kfb twice, k3, ssk, k2tog, k3] 7 times, kfb.
Rnd 3 Knit.
Rnd 4 Rep rnd 2.
Break B, join A.
Rnd 5 Knit.
Rnds 6–8 Rep rnds 2–4.
Rep rnds 5–8 for 6 times more, working 4 rnds in each color in foll sequence: E, D, C, A, E, and A.
Next 2 rnds With E, knit.
Bottom
Rnd 1 *K6, k2tog; rep from * around—84 sts.
Rnd 2 and all even-numbered rnds Knit.
Rnd 3 *K5, k2tog; rep from * around—72 sts.
Rnd 5 *K4, k2tog; rep from * around—60 sts.
Next 2 rnds Knit.

FINISHING
Turn piece inside out and divide sts in half with 30 sts on each end of the circular needle. With spare needle, use 3-needle bind-off to seam the bottom.❖

soft wear

A basic tube sock becomes a luxury item
when it's knit in snuggly soft angora.

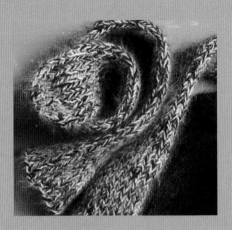

WHAT YOU NEED

Yarn
Angora Fashion **by Schulana/Skacel
Collection, .88oz/25g skeins, each approx
122yd/112m (angora/nylon)** ③
• **2 balls each in #01 white (A) and
#08 black (B) (version 1) OR 3 balls in #13
purple (version 2)**

Needles
• **One set (4) size 6 (4mm) double-pointed
needles (dpns)** or size to obtain gauge

Notions
• **Stitch marker**

Skill Level

●●○○

ANGORA TUBE SOCKS

Looking for a quick-to-make, luxurious
gift? Whip up some angora bed socks,
given here in two lengths. The yarn is held
double, which ups the plush quotient and
knitting speed, and wears better over time.
Originally this design had a shaped heel,
but the long-haired fibers looked matted—
angora works better in the continuous
structure of a tube sock, as does any very
textured yarn. Unworn, the foot looks nar-
row because of the ribbing, but it provides
for a snugger fit. Don't forget to attach a
gift tag noting that these lovelies should
be cold-water washed and hung to dry.

SIZES

Instructions are written for size
Small/Medium (Woman's shoe sizes 5–8).
Changes for Large (Woman's shoe sizes
9–10) are in parentheses.

FINISHED MEASUREMENTS

Circumference (unstretched) 5 (7)"/12.5 (18)cm
Length (version 1) 24 (25)"/61 (63.5)cm
Length (version 2) 15½ (16½)"/39 (40.5)cm

GAUGES

16 sts and 22 rnds to 4"/10cm over St st
using size 6 (4mm) needles and 2 strands
of yarn held tog.
20 sts and 22 rnds to 4"/10cm over k1, p1 rib
using size 6 (4mm) needles and 2 strands of
yarn held tog. **Take time to check gauges.**

WRAP (OR TURKISH) CAST-ON

Hold 2 dpns parallel. Beg with tail of yarn at
LH side and in front of needles, wrap the
working yarn around both needles for half
the number of sts to cast on. (Wrap 6 times to
cast on 12 sts.) Bring the yarn to the front
between the needles to knit the sts on the top
needle with a 3rd dpn. Rotate the needles to
knit the rem sts with free dpn.

K1, P1 RIB

(over an even number of sts)
Rnd 1 *K1, p1; rep from * around.
Rep rnd 1 for k1, p1 rib.

SOCKS

With 1 strand each of A and B (version 1)
or 2 strands of C held tog (version 2), cast
on 12 sts using the wrap method.
Toe
Rnd 1 and all odd-numbered rnds Knit.
Rnd 2 *K1, kfb; rep from * around—18 sts.
Rnd 4 *K2, kfb; rep from * around—24 sts.
Rnd 6 *K3, kfb; rep from * around—30 sts.

For size Medium/Large only
Rnd 8 *K4, kfb; rep from * around—36 sts.

For both sizes
Foot/leg
Rnd 1 Knit.
Work in k1, p1 rib until sock measures
24 (25)"/61 (63.5)cm for version 1 or
15½ (16½)"/39 (40.5)cm for version 2.
Bind off loosely in pat. ✤

fur sure

Two yarns in soft cream show off
the interplay between textured stitches and fun fur.

fur sure

WHAT YOU NEED

Yarn
Comfort Sock **by Berroco Yarns, 3½oz/100g skeins, each approx 447yd/412m (nylon/acrylic)** (1)
• **2 skeins in #1702 pearl (B)**
Plume **by Prism Arts, 2.8oz/79g hanks, each approx 45yd/41m (nylon)** (6)
• **1 hank in pearl (A)**

Needles
• **One set (4) sizes 6 and 9 (4 and 5.5mm) double-pointed needles (dpns)** or size to obtain gauge

Notions
• **Cable needle (cn)**
• **Stitch marker**
• **Scrap yarn**

Skill Level
●●●○

TEXTURE AND FUR SOCKS

I love using a variety of textures in one design. Here is one with a fluffy yarn (Prism's **Plume**) to contrast with Berroco's smooth **Comfort Sock**, which shows off cables beautifully. I like to keep the colors monochromatic so that the textures jump out more, but of course creative color-blocking can be just as fun.

SIZES

Instructions are written for Medium/Large (Woman's shoe sizes 7–10).

FINISHED MEASUREMENTS

Foot circumference 7"/18cm
Length from heel to toe 10"/25.5cm
Length from cuff to bottom of foot 11"/28cm

GAUGES

12 sts and 16 rnds to 4"/10cm over St st using larger needles and A.
20 sts and 28 rnds to 4"/10cm over St st using smaller needles and 2 strands of B held tog. **Take time to check gauges.**

WRAP (OR TURKISH) CAST-ON

Hold 2 dpns parallel. Beg with tail of yarn at LH side and in front of needles, wrap the working yarn around both needles for half the number of sts to cast on. (Wrap 6 times to cast on 12 sts.) Bring the yarn to the front between the needles to knit the sts on the top needle with a 3rd dpn. Rotate the needles to knit the rem sts with free dpn.

RIBBED CABLE PATTERN

(over 22 sts)
Rnds 1–6 P1, k1 tbl, p1, k1, [p2, k2] 3 times, p2, k1, p1, k1 tbl, p1.
Rnd 7 P1, k1 tbl, p1, sl 4 sts to cn and hold to **back**, k1, p2, k1; then k1, p2, k1 from cn, sl 4 sts to cn and hold to **front**, k1, p2, k1; then k1, p2, k1 from cn, p1, k1 tbl, p1.
Rnds 8–10 Rep rnd 1.
Rep rnds 1–10 for ribbed cable pat.

NOTE

The sock is worked from the toe up with the cuff worked inside out. This is to allow the maximum amount of "wisps" to be on the outside of the sock. If desired, the remaining wisps can be pushed to the outside of the sock with the point of a knitting needle.

SOCKS

With 2 strands of B held tog and smaller dpns, cast on 12 sts using the wrap method and divide evenly on 3 dpns. Pm for beg of rnd.
Toe
Rnd 1 Knit, placing 12 sts on N1 and 6 sts each on N2 and N3.
Rnd 2 With N1, k1, kfb, k to last 2 sts, kfb, k1; with N2, k1, kfb, knit to end; with N3, k to last 2 sts, kfb, k1—28 sts.
Rnd 3 Knit.
Rep rnds 4 and 5 for 7 times more—44 sts; 22 sts on N1, 11 sts each on N2 and N3.
Next rnd Work ribbed cable pat over 22 sts, k to end of rnd. Cont to work in this manner, rep rnds 1–10 of ribbed cable pat until piece measures 9"/23cm or 2"/5cm less than desired length from heel to toe.
Afterthought heel setup
Next rnd With N1, work in pat. With N2 and N3, with scrap yarn, knit, sl scrap yarn sts back to LH needle and knit again with 2 strands of B held tog.
Work even in pats as established for 3"/7.5cm more.
Leg
Turn the sock inside out to work cuff from WS. Change to larger needles.
Rnd 1 With single strand of A, knit.
Rnd 2 K2tog around—22 sts.
Rnd 3 With 2 strands of B held tog, kfb around—44 sts.
Rnds 4 and 5 *K1, p1; rep from * around.
Rep rnds 2–5 for 10 times more.
Bind off loosely in pat. Turn sock right side out. Change to smaller needles.
Afterthought heel
Remove scrap yarn from heel, placing sts on 3 dpns as foll: 22 sts on N1, 11 sts each on N2 and N3.
Rnd 1 With 2 strands of B held tog, knit.
Rnd 2 With N1, k1, ssk, k to last 3 sts, k2tog, k1; with N2, k1, ssk, k to end; with N3, k to last 3 sts, k2tog, k1—4 sts dec'd.
Rep last 2 rnds 7 times more—12 sts.
Divide sts evenly on 2 dpns and graft heel closed using Kitchener st.✤

the joy of socks

Put your leftover yarn to good use with this
sweet garland of mini socks that can be knit top-down or toe-up.

WHAT YOU NEED

Yarn

Leftover sock yarn **in at least two colors (A for main color and B for trim color) for each mini sock (sample is made up of 18 mini socks)** (**1**)

Needles

• **One set (4) size 2 (2.75mm) double-pointed needles (dpns)** or size to obtain gauge

Notions

• **Stitch marker**
• **Scrap yarn to attach socks to sisal and for afterthought heel setup**
• **1 small jingle bell for each sock**
• **10yd/10m sisal twine**

Skill Level

● ● ○ ○

FINISHED MEASUREMENTS

Length from heel to toe 3"/7.5cm
Length from cuff to heel 2"/6.5cm
Length of garland 1½–2yd/1.5–2m

GAUGE

28 sts and 40 rnds to 4"/10cm over St st using size 2 (2.75mm) needles. **Take time to check gauge.**

K1, P1 RIB

(over an even number of sts)
Rnd 1 *K1, p1; rep from * around.
Rep rnd 1 for k1, p1 rib.

MINI SOCKS (VERSION 1: TOP-DOWN WITH HEEL FLAP/GUSSET)

With B, cast on 24 sts and divide on 3 dpns as foll: 12 sts on N1; 6 sts each on N2 and N3. Pm for beg of rnd and join, being careful not to twist sts.

Cuff
Rnds 1–6 Knit. Break B.
Leg
Rnds 1–13 With A, knit.
Heel flap
Work back and forth on N1 only as foll:
Row 1 (RS) K2tog, * sl 1, k1; rep from * to last st, k1—11 sts.
Row 2 (WS) Purl.
Row 3 *K1, sl 1; rep from *, end k1.
Row 4 Purl.
Rows 5–10 Rep rows 3 and 4 for 3 times more.
Gusset
Next rnd With N1, kfb, k to end, pick up and k 6 sts along edge of heel flap; with N2, k12; with N3, pick up and k 6 sts along edge of heel flap, then k6 from N1, pm for new beg of rnd—36 sts.
Rnd 1 With N1, k to last 3 sts, k2tog, k1; with N2, knit; with N3, k1, ssk, k to end—34 sts.
Rnd 2 Knit.
Rep rnds 1 and 2 for 5 times more—24 sts.
Foot
Rnds 1–8 Knit.

Toe

Rnd 1 With N1, k to last 3 sts, k2tog, k2; with N2, k1, ssk, k to last 3 sts, k2tog, k1; with N3, k1, ssk, k to end—20 sts.
Rnd 2 Knit.
Rep rnds 1 and 2 for 3 times more—8 sts.
Next rnd K2tog around.
Break yarn, leaving a 6"/15cm tail; thread tail through rem sts.

FINISHING

Attach jingle bell to toe.

MINI SOCKS (VERSION 2: TOE-UP WITH AFTERTHOUGHT HEEL)

With B, cast on 24 sts and divide on 3 dpns as foll: 12 sts on N1, 6 sts each on N2 and N3. Pm for beg of rnd and join, being careful not to twist sts.
Cuff
Rnds 1–8 Work in k1, p1 rib. Break B.
Leg
Rnds 1–13 With A, knit.
Afterthought heel setup
Next rnd With scrap yarn, k12, sl scrap yarn sts back to LH needle and knit them again with A.
Foot
Rnds 1–14 Knit.
Toe
Work as for version 1.
Afterthought heel
Remove scrap yarn from heel and place 24 sts on 3 needles so 12 sts from bottom of heel are on N2, and 12 sts from top of heel are divided evenly on N1 and N3. With A, work as for toe.

FINISHING

Attach jingle bell to toe.

GARLAND

With sisal, make a hanging loop at the beginning of the twine. With scrap yarn, attach a mini sock every 5"/13cm or so. Make another hanging loop at end. ✤

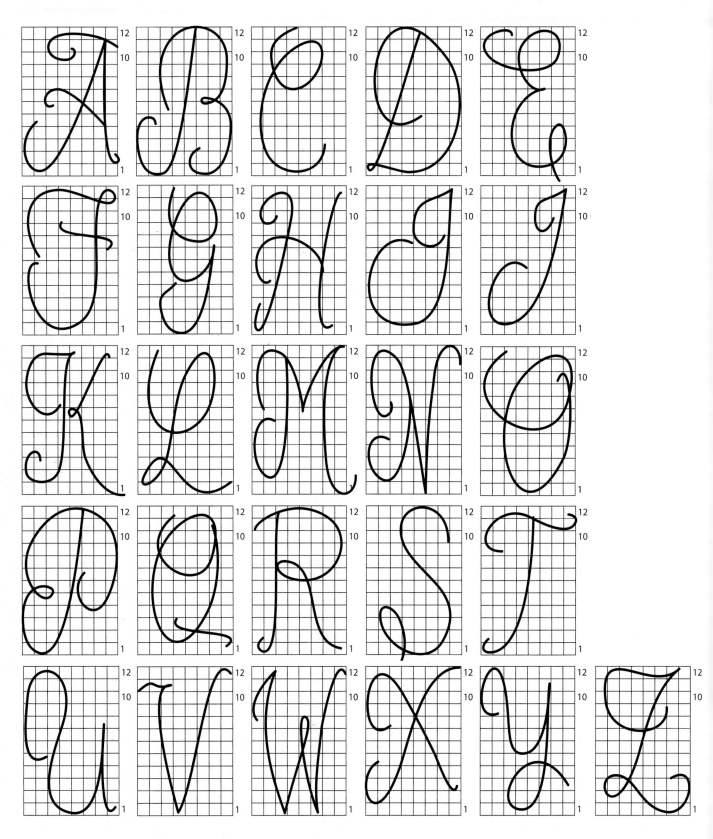

tools, tips, & techniques

back to basics

Master three types of construction
while creating a perennial classic: the simple ankle sock.

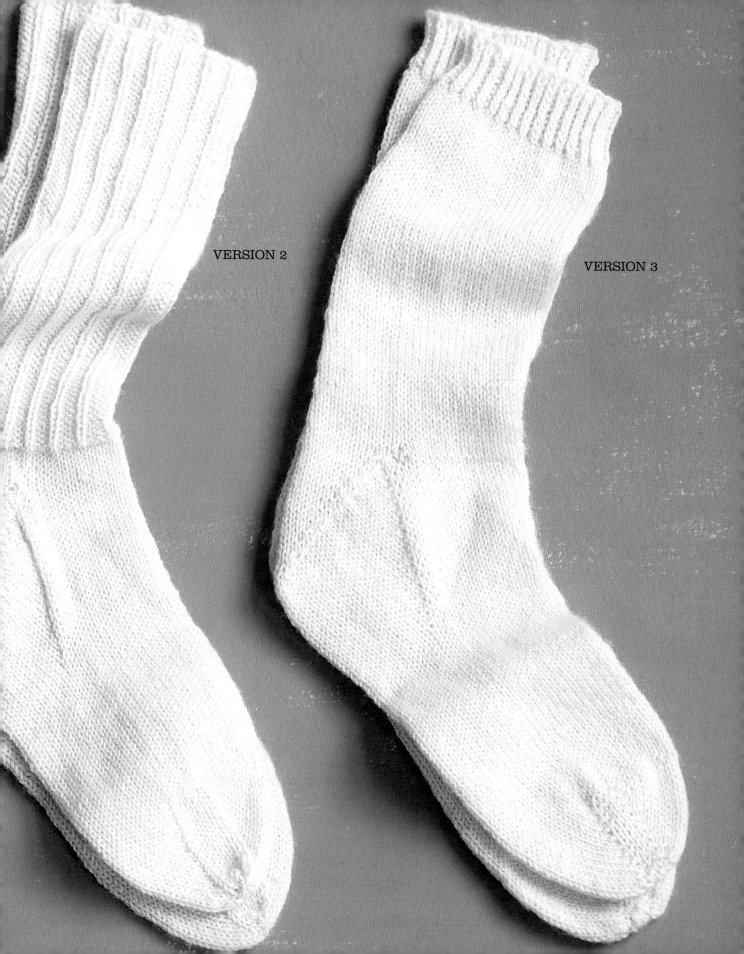

VERSION 2

VERSION 3

WHAT YOU NEED

Yarn
Regia 4-ply **by Schachenmayr Regia,**
1¾oz/50g skeins, each approx 230yd/210m
(wool/polyamide) (**1**)
• **2 skeins in #00600 white**

Needles
• **One set (4) size 2 (2.75mm) double-pointed needles (dpns)** or size to obtain gauge

Notions
• **Stitch marker**
• **Scrap yarn**

Skill Level
●●○○

CLASSIC ANKLE SOCKS

Get the same look with three different construction techniques: (1) cuff-down with afterthought heel, (2) cuff down with heel flap and gusset, or (3) toe-up with heel flap and gusset.

SIZE

Instructions are written for size Medium/Large (Woman's shoe sizes 7–10).

FINISHED MEASUREMENTS

Foot circumference 7"/18cm
Length from back of heel to toe 8¾"/12.25cm
Length from bottom of heel to top 10"/25.5cm

GAUGE

32 sts and 40 rnds to 4"/10cm over St st using size 2 (2.75mm) needles. **Take time to check gauge.**

TWISTED RIB

(over an even number of sts)
Rnd 1 *K1 tbl, p1; rep from * around.
Rep rnd 1 for twisted rib.

K2, P2 RIB

(multiple of 4 sts)
Rnd 1 *K2, p2; rep from * around.
Rep rnd 1 for k2, p2 rib.

P3, K1 RIB

(multiple of 4 sts)
Rnd 1 *P3, k1; rep from * around.
Rep rnd 1 for p3, k1 rib.

WRAP (OR TURKISH) CAST-ON

Hold 2 dpns parallel. Beg with tail of yarn at LH side and in front of needles, wrap the working yarn around both needles for half the number of sts to cast on. (Wrap 6 times to cast on 12 sts.) Bring the yarn to the front between the needles to knit the sts on the top needle with a 3rd dpn. Rotate the needles to knit the rem sts with free dpn.

ANKLE SOCKS, VERSION 1
(CUFF DOWN WITH AFTERTHOUGHT HEEL)

Cuff
Cast on 56 sts and divide on 3 dpns as foll: 28 sts on N1; 14 sts each on N2 and N3. Pm for beg of rnd and join, being careful not to twist sts.
Work in k2, p2 rib for 7"/18cm.
Knit 6 rnds.
Afterthought heel setup
Next rnd With N1, knit; with N2 and N3

and scrap yarn, k28, return scrap yarn sts to LH needle and knit them again with working yarn.
Work even in St st until foot measures 6"/15cm or 2"/5cm less than desired length from scrap yarn.
Toe shaping
Next rnd With N1, k1, ssk, k to last 3 sts, k2tog, k1; with N2, k1, ssk, k to end; with N3, k to last 3 sts, k2tog, k1—4 sts dec'd.
Knit 1 rnd.
Rep last 2 rnds for 8 times more, then rep dec rnd once more—16 sts.
Divide sts evenly on 2 dpns. Graft toe closed using Kitchener st.
Afterthought heel
Remove scrap yarn, placing 28 sts on N1 and 14 sts each on N2 and N3. Work as for toe until 12 sts rem. Divide sts evenly on 2 dpns. Graft toe closed using Kitchener st.

ANKLE SOCKS, VERSION 2
(CUFF DOWN WITH HEEL FLAP & GUSSET)

Cuff
Cast on 56 sts and divide on 3 dpn as foll: 28 sts on N1, 14 sts each on N2 and N3. Pm for beg of rnd and join, being careful not to twist sts.
Work in p3, k1 rib until piece measures 8¼"/21cm from beg.
Knit 6 rnds.
Heel flap
Next rnd With N1, kfb, k27; with N2 and N3, knit—57 sts.
Work back and forth on the 29 sts on N1 only as foll:
Row 1 (RS) *k1, sl 1; rep from *, end k1.
Row 2 (WS) Purl.
Rep rows 1 and 2 until heel flap measures 1½"/3.5cm.
Next row (RS) *K1, sl 1; rep from * to last 2 sts, k2tog—28 sts.
Instep
Next rnd With N1, pick up and k 12 sts along edge of heel flap; with N2, k28 (for instep); with N3, pick up and k 12 sts along edge of heel flap, then knit first 14 sts from N1, pm for new beg of rnd—80 sts.
Knit one rnd.
Gusset
Rnd 1 With N1, k to last 4 sts, k2tog, k2; with N2, knit; with N3, k2, ssk, k to end—2 sts dec'd.
Rnd 2 Knit.
Rep last 2 rnds for 11 times more—56 sts.
Work even in St st until foot measures

5¼"/14cm or 2"/5cm less than desired sock length.

Work toe as for version 1 to complete sock.

ANKLE SOCKS, VERSION 3
(TOE UP WITH HEEL FLAP & GUSSET)

Toe

Cast on 12 sts using the wrap method. Pm for beg of rnd.

Rnd 1 Knit.

Rnd 2 Kfb around—24 sts.

Rnd 3 Knit. Arrange sts on dpns as foll: 12 sts on N1, 6 sts each on N2 and N3.

Rnd 4 With N1, k1, kfb, k to last 2 sts, kfb, k1; with N2, k1, kfb, k to end; with N3, k until to last 2 sts, kfb, k1—4 sts inc'd.

Rnd 5 Knit.

Rep rnds 4 and 5 for 7 times more—56 sts. Work even in St st until sock measures 6¼"/16cm or 2½"/6.5cm less than desired sock length.

Gusset

Rnd 1 With N1, knit; with N2, k1, kfb, k to end; with N3, k to last 2 sts, kfb, k1—4 sts inc'd.

Rnd 2 Knit.

Rep rnds 1 and 2 for 11 times more—80 sts, 28 sts on N1, 26 sts each on N2 and N3.

Turn heel

Next (dec) rnd With N1, knit; with N2, k to last 4 sts, ssk, k2; with N3, k2, k2tog, k1. Turn to work back and forth on N2 and N3 only.

Row 2 (WS) With N3, p4; with N2, p2, p2tog, p1. Turn.

Row 3 (RS) with N2, k4; with N3, k3, k2tog, k1. Turn.

Row 4 With N3, p5; with N2, p3, p2tog, p1. Turn.

Row 5 With N2, k5; with N3, k4, k2tog, k1. Turn.

Row 6 With N3, p6; with N2, p4, p2tog, p1. Turn.

Row 7 With N2, k6; with N2, k5, k2tog, k1. Turn.

Row 8 With N3, p7; with N2, p5, p2tog, p1. Turn.

Cont in this manner until all sts on heel have been worked and 28 sts rem on N2 and N3.

Ankle

Resume working in the rnd and work in St st for 6½"/16.5cm or 1"/2.5cm less than desired length.

Work in twisted rib for 1"/2.5cm. Bind off loosely in pat.✤

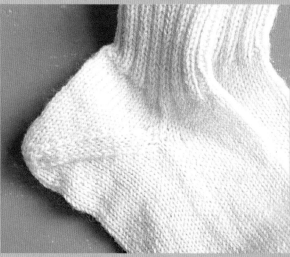

VERSION 1

VERSION 2

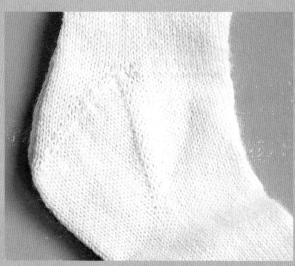

VERSION 3

abbreviations

approx	approximately
beg	begin(ning)
CC	contrasting color
ch	chain
cm	centimeter(s)
cn	cable needle
cont	continu(e)(ing)
dec	decreas(e)(ing)
dpn(s)	double-pointed needle(s)
foll	follow(s)(ing)
g	gram(s)
inc	increas(e)(ing)
k	knit
kfb	knit into the front and back of a stitch—one stitch has been increased
k2tog	knit 2 stitches together—one stitch has been decreased
LH	left-hand
lp(s)	loop(s)
m	meter(s)
mm	millimeter(s)
MC	main color
M1 or M1L	make one or make one left (see glossary)
M1 p-st	make 1 purl stitch (see glossary)
M1R	make one right (see glossary)
N1 (N2, N3)	needle 1 (2, 3)
oz	ounce(s)
p	purl
pat(s)	pattern(s)
pm	place marker (see glossary)
psso	pass slip stitch(es) over
p2tog	purl two stitches together—one stitch has been decreased
rem	remain(s)(ing)
rep	repeat
RH	right-hand
RS	right side(s)
rnd(s)	round(s)
SKP	slip 1, knit 1, pass slip stitch over—one stitch has been decreased
SK2P	slip 1, knit 2 together, pass slipped stitch over the knit 2 together—two stitches have been decreased
S2KP	slip 2 stitches together, knit 1, pass 2 slipped stitches over knit 1—two stitches have been decreased
sl	slip
sl st	slip stitch (see glossary)
ssk	slip, slip, knit (see glossary)
sssk	slip, slip, slip, knit (see glossary)
st(s)	stitch(es)
St st	stockinette stitch
tbl	through the back loop(s)
tog	together
WS	wrong side(s)
wyib	with yarn in back
wyif	with yarn in front
yd	yard(s)
yo	yarn over needle (U.K.: see glossary)
*	repeat directions following * as many times as indicated

knitting needles

U.S.	Metric
0	2mm
1	2.25mm
2	2.75mm
3	3.25mm
4	3.5mm
5	3.75mm
6	4mm
7	4.5mm
8	5mm
9	5.5mm
10	6mm
10½	6.5mm
11	8mm
13	9mm
15	10mm
17	12.75mm
19	15mm
35	19mm

skill levels for knitting

●○○○ ●●○○ ●●●○ ●●●●

Beginner
Ideal first project.

Easy
Basic stitches, minimal shaping, simple finishing.

Intermediate
For knitters with some experience. More intricate stitches, shaping, and finishing.

Experienced
For knitters able to work patterns with complicated shaping and finishing.

standard yarn weight system

Categories of yarn, gauge ranges, and recommended needle and hook sizes

Yarn Weight Symbol & Category Names	0 Lace	1 Super Fine	2 Fine	3 Light	4 Medium	5 Bulky	6 Super Bulky
Type of Yarns in Category	Fingering 10 count crochet thread	Sock, Fingering, Baby	Sport, Baby	DK, Light Worsted	Worsted, Afghan, Aran	Chunky, Craft, Rug	Bulky, Roving
Knit Gauge Range* in Stockinette Stitch to 4 inches	33 –40** sts	27–32 sts	23–26 sts	21–24 sts	16–20 sts	12–15 sts	6–11 sts
Recommended Needle in Metric Size Range	1.5–2.25 mm	2.25–3.25 mm	3.25–3.75 mm	3.75—4.5 mm	4.5–5.5 mm	5.5–8 mm	8 mm and larger
Recommended Needle U.S. Size Range	000 to 1	1 to 3	3 to 5	5 to 7	7 to 9	9 to 11	11 and larger
Crochet Gauge* Ranges in Single Crochet to 4 inch	32-42 double crochets**	21–32 sts	16–20 sts	12–17 sts	11–14 sts	8–11 sts	5–9 sts
Recommended Hook in Metric Size Range	Steel*** 1.6–1.4mm Regular hook 2.25 mm	2.25–3.5 mm	3.5–4.5 mm	4.5–5.5 mm	5.5–6.5 mm	6.5–9 mm	9 mm and larger
Recommended Hook U.S. Size Range	Steel*** 6, 7, 8 Regular hook B–1	B–1 to E–4	E–4 to 7	7 to I–9	I–9 to K–10½	K–10½ to M–13	M–13 and larger

* Guidelines only: The above reflect the most commonly used gauges and needle or hook sizes for specific yarn categories.

** Lace weight yarns are usually knitted or crocheted on larger needles and hooks to create lacy, openwork patterns. Accordingly, a gauge range is difficult to determine. Always follow the gauge stated in your pattern.

*** Steel crochet hooks are sized differently from regular hooks—the higher the number, the smaller the hook, which is the reverse of regular hook sizing.

gauge

Make a test swatch at least 4"/10cm square. If the number of stitches and rows does not correspond to the gauge given, change your needle size. An easy rule to follow is: To get fewer stitches to the inch/cm, use a larger needle; to get more stitches to the inch/cm, use a smaller needle. Continue to try different needle sizes until you get the correct number of stitches in the gauge.

Rows measured over 4"/5cm.

Stitches measured over 4"/5cm.

metric conversions

To convert from inches to centimeters, simply multiply by 2.54.

glossary

bind off Used to finish an edge or segment. Lift the first stitch over the second, the second over the third, etc. (U.K.: cast off)

bind off in rib or pat Work in rib or pat as you bind off. (Knit the knit stitches, purl the purl stitches.)

cast on Place a foundation row of stitches upon the needle in order to begin knitting.

decrease Reduce the stitches in a row (for example, knit two together).

increase Add stitches in a row (for example, knit in front and back of stitch).

knitwise Insert the needle into the stitch as if you were going to knit it.

make one or make one left Insert left-hand needle from front to back under the strand between last st worked and next st on left-hand needle. Knit into the back loop to twist the stitch.

make one p-st Insert needle from front to back under the strand between the last stitch worked and the next stitch on the left-hand needle. Purl into the back loop to twist the stitch.

make one right Insert left-hand needle from back to front under the strand between the last stitch worked and the next stitch on left-hand needle. Knit into the front loop to twist the stitch.

no stitch On some charts, "no stitch" is indicated with shaded spaces where stitches have been decreased or not yet made. In such cases, work the stitches of the chart, skipping over the "no stitch" spaces.

place marker Place or attach a loop of contrast yarn or purchased stitch marker as indicated.

pick up and knit (purl) Knit (or purl) into the loops along an edge.

purlwise Insert the needle into the stitch as if you were going to purl it.

selvage stitch Edge stitch that helps make seaming easier.

slip, slip, knit Slip next two stitches knitwise, one at a time, to right-hand needle. Insert tip of left-hand needle into fronts of these stitches, from left to right. Knit them together. One stitch has been decreased.

slip, slip, slip, knit Slip next three stitches knitwise, one at a time, to right-hand needle. Insert tip of left-hand needle into fronts of these stitches, from left to right. Knit them together. Two stitches have been decreased.

slip stitch An unworked stitch made by passing a stitch from the left-hand to the right-hand needle as if to purl.

work even Continue in pattern without increasing or decreasing. (U.K.: work straight)

yarn over Make a new stitch by wrapping the yarn over the right-hand needle. (U.K.: yfwd, yon, yrn)

sockets
(page 46)

basic stitches

garter stitch (flat)
Knit every row.

garter stitch (in the round)
Knit one round, then purl one round.

stockinette stitch (flat)
Knit right-side rows and purl wrong-side rows.

stockinette stitch (in the round)
Knit every round.

reverse stockinette stitch (flat)
Purl right-side rows and knit wrong-side rows.

reverse stockinette stitch (in the round)
Purl every round.

seed stitch
Row 1 (RS) *Knit one, purl one; repeat from * to end.
Row 2 Knit the purl stitches and purl the knit stitches. Repeat row 2 for seed stitch.

essential techniques

knitting with circular needles

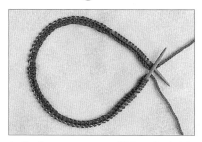 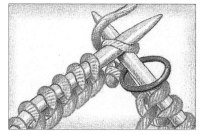 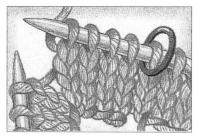

1. Cast on as you would for straight knitting. Distribute the stitches evenly around the needle, being sure not to twist them. The last cast-on stitch is the last stitch of the round. Place a marker here to indicate the end of the round.

2. Hold the needle tip with the last cast-on stitch in your right hand and the tip with the first cast-on stitch in your left hand. Knit the first cast-on stitch, pulling the yarn tight to avoid a gap.

3. Work until you reach the marker. This completes the first round. Slip the marker to the right needle and work the next round.

knitting with double-pointed needles

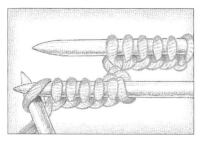 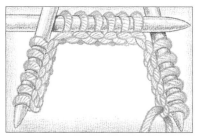 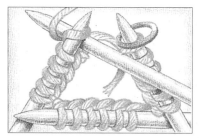

1. Cast on a third of the required stitches on the first needle, plus one. Slip this extra stitch to the next needle as shown. Continue in this way on the second and third needles.

2. Arrange the needles as shown, with the cast-on edge facing the center of the triangle (or square, if four needles).

3. Place a marker after the last cast-on stitch. With the free needle, knit the first cast-on stitch, pulling tightly. Continue in rounds, slipping the marker.

the net set
(page 22)

in the bag
(page 130)

layer cake
(page 90)

Kitchener stitch (grafting)

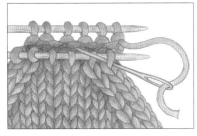

1. Insert tapestry needle purlwise (as shown) through first stitch on front needle. Pull yarn through, leaving that stitch on needle.

2. Insert tapestry needle knitwise (as shown) through first stitch on back needle. Pull yarn through, leaving stitch on needle.

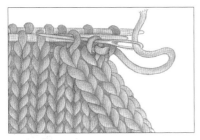

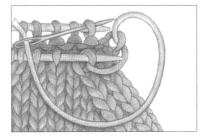

3. Insert tapestry needle knitwise through first stitch on front needle, slip stitch off needle and insert tapestry needle purlwise (as shown) through next stitch on front needle. Pull yarn through, leaving this stitch on needle.

4. Insert tapestry needle purlwise through first stitch on back needle. Slip stitch off needle and insert tapestry needle knitwise (as shown) through next stitch on back needle. Pull yarn through, leaving this stitch on needle.
Repeat steps 3 and 4 until all stitches on both front and back needles have been grafted. Fasten off and weave in end.

chain stitch embroidery

Draw the needle up and *insert it back where it just came out, taking a short stitch. With the needle above the yarn, hold the yarn with your thumb and draw it through. Repeat from *.

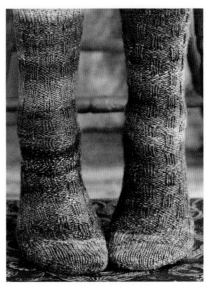

dyed in the wool
(page 122)

letter perfect
(page 62)

picking up stitches along a horizontal edge

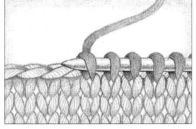

1. Insert the knitting needle into the center of the first stitch in the row below the bound-off edge. Wrap the yarn knitwise around the needle.

2. Draw the yarn through. You have picked up one stitch. Continue to pick up one stitch in each stitch along the bound-off edge.

picking up stitches along a vertical edge

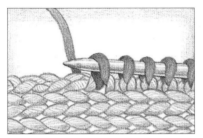

1. Insert the knitting needle into the corner stitch of the first row, one stitch in from the side edge. Wrap the yarn around the needle knitwise.

2. Draw the yarn through. You have picked up one stitch. Continue to pick up stitches along the edge. Occasionally skip one row to keep the edge from flaring.

picking up stitches with a crochet hook

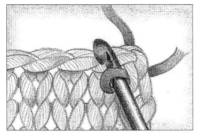

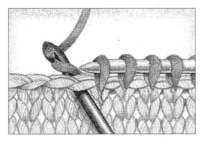

1. Insert the crochet hook from front to back into the center of the first stitch one row below the bound-off edge. Catch the yarn and pull a loop through.

2. Slip the loop onto the knitting needle, being sure it is not twisted. Continue to pick up one stitch in each stitch along the bound-off edge.

garden variety
(page 110)

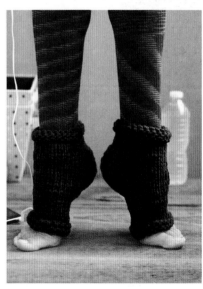

sweet tee
(page 126)

Fair Isle stranding: one-handed

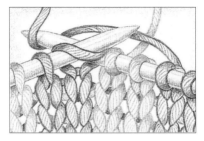

1. Drop the working yarn. Bring the new color (now the working yarn) over the top of the dropped yarn and work to the next color change.

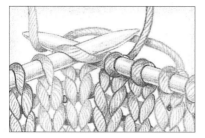

2. Drop the working yarn. Bring the new color under the dropped yarn and work to the next color change. Repeat steps 1 and 2.

Fair Isle stranding: two-handed

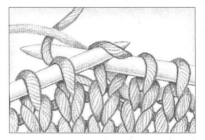

1. Hold the working yarn in your right hand and the non-working yarn in your left hand. Bring the working yarn over the top of the yarn in your left hand and knit with the right hand to the next color change.

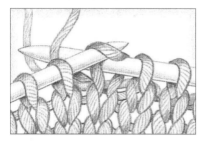

2. The yarn in your right hand is now the non-working yarn; the yarn in your left hand is the working yarn. Bring the working yarn under the non-working yarn and knit with the left and to the next color change. Repeat steps 1 and 2.

yarn over between two knit stitches

Bring the yarn from the back of the work to the front between the two needles. Knit the next stitch, bringing the yarn to the back over the right needle as shown.

Bring the yarn from the back to the front between the two needles, then to the back over the right needle and to the front again as shown. Purl the next stitch.

festive feet
(page 102)

with bells on
(page 34)

left (or front) cable

 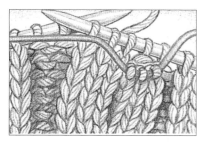 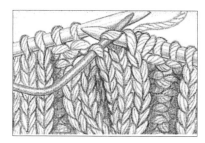

1. Slip the first three stitches of the cable purlwise to a cable needle and hold them to the front of the work. Be careful not to twist the stitches.

2. Leave the stitches suspended in front of the work, keeping them in the center of the cable needle where they won't slip off. Pull the yarn firmly and knit the next three stitches.

3. Knit the three stitches from the cable needle. If this seems too awkward, return the stitches to the left needle and then knit them.

right (or back) cable

 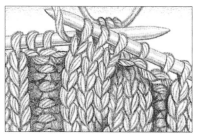 

1. Slip the first three stitches of the cable purlwise to a cable needle and hold them to the back of the work. Be careful not to twist the stitches.

2. Leave the stitches suspended in back of the work, keeping them in the center of the cable needle where they won't slip off. Pull the yarn firmly and knit the next three stitches.

3. Knit the three stitches from the cable needle. If this seems too awkward, return the stitches to the left needle and then knit them.

bob & weave
(page 74)

all in the family
(page 82)

fur sure
(page 136)

long-tail cast-on

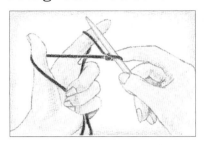

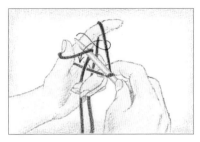

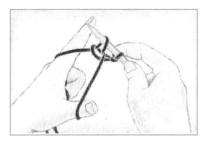

1. Make a slip knot on the right needle, leaving a long tail. wind the tail end around your left thumb, front to back. Wrap the yarn from the ball over your left index finger and secure the ends in your palm.

2. Insert the needle upward in the loop on your thumb. Then, with the needle, draw the yarn from the ball through the loop to form a stitch.

3. Take your thumb out of the loop and tighten the loop on the needle. Continue in this way until the required number of stitches are cast on.

crochet chain

1. Pass yarn over hook and catch with hook.

2. Draw yarn through loop on hook.

3. Repeat steps 1 and 2 to make chain.

pom queen
(page 42)

do the twist
(page 38)

ribs with sauce
(page 70)

resources

Be Sweet
1315 Bridgeway
Sausalito, CA 94965
www.besweetproducts.com

Berroco, Inc.
1 Tupperware Drive, Suite 4
North Smithfield, RI
02896-6815
www.berroco.com

Brown Sheep Company
100662 County Road 16
Mitchell, NE 69357
www.brownsheep.com

Bryson Distributing
brysonknits.com

Cartwright's Sequins
www.ccartwright.com

Cascade Yarns
1224 Andover Park East
Tukwila, WA 98188
www.cascadeyarns.com

Classic Elite Yarns
122 Western Avenue
Lowell, MA 01851
www.classiceliteyarns.com

Debbie Bliss
Distributed by Knitting Fever (KFI)
www.debbieblissonline.com

Fire Mountain Gems
1 Fire Mountain Way
Grants Pass, OR 97526
www.firemountaingems.com

Knitting Fever (KFI)
P.O. Box 336
315 Bayview Avenue
Amityville, NY 11701
www.knittingfever.com

Koigu Wool Designs
P.O. Box 158
Chatsworth, ON
N0H 1G0 Canada
www.koigu.com

Lorna's Laces
4229 N. Honore St.
Chicago, IL 60613
www.lornaslaces.net

Louet North America
3425 Hands Rd,
Prescott, ON
K0E 1T0 Canada
www.louet.com

Madelinetosh
7515 Benbrook Pkwy
Benbrook, TX 76126
madelinetosh.com

Misti Alpaca Yarns
In the U.S.:
P.O. Box 2532
Glen Ellyn, IL 60138
www.mistialpaca.com
In Canada:
Old Mill Knitting Company
F.G. P.O. Box 81176
Ancaster, ON
L9G 4X2 Canada
www.oldmillknitting.com

Noro
Distributed by Knitting Fever (KFI)

Quince & Co.
www.quinceandco.com

Schachenmayr Regia
us.schachenmayr.com/regia

Schulana
Distributed by Skacel
Collection, Inc.

Skacel Collection, Inc.
www.skacelknitting.com

Spud & Chloë
Blue Sky Alpacas
Attn: Spud & Chloë
P.O. Box 88
Cedar, MN 55011
www.spudandchloe.com

Tanglewood Fiber Creations
www.tanglewoodfibercreations.com

index